Office Weapons

Office Weapons

Catapults, Darts, Shooters, Tripwires, and Other Do-It-Yourself Projects to Fortify your Cubicle

Edited by Mike Warren

Skyhorse Publishing

Skyhorse Publishing books may be purchased in bulk at special discounts for sales promotion, corporate gifts, fund-raising, or educational purposes. Special editions can also be created to specifications. For details, contact the Special Sales Department, Skyhorse Publishing, 307 West 36th Street, 11th Floor, New York, NY 10018 or info@skyhorsepublishing.com.

Skyhorse® and Skyhorse Publishing® are registered trademarks of Skyhorse Publishing, Inc.®, a Delaware corporation.

www.skyhorsepublishing.com

10 9 8 7 6 5 4 3 2 1

Library of Congress Cataloging-in-Publication is available on file.

ISBN: 978-1-62087-708-1

Printed in China

Disclaimer:

This book is intended to offer general guidance. It is sold with the understanding that every effort was made to provide the most current and accurate information. However, errors and omissions are still possible. Any use or misuse of the information contained herein is solely the responsibility of the user, and the author and publisher make no warrantees or claims as to the truth or validity of the information. The author and publisher shall have neither liability nor responsibility to any person or entity with respect to any loss or damage caused, or alleged to have been caused, directly or indirectly, by the information contained in this book. Furthermore, this book is not intended to give professional dietary, technical, or medical advice. Please refer to and follow any local laws when using any of the information contained herein, and act responsibly and safely at all times.

Table of Contents

table of contents

Introduction

It's war!!

If you've spent any time in a cubicle, you know that there are times when you might need to fashion some kind of weapon out of office supplies. Maybe you're waging war on your cubicle neighbor, or simply defending your domain from the devious IT department; whatever your office turmoil, *Office Weapons* has got you covered. This collection of weaponry are made from easy to find supplies, and can be found in many offices. And, in the spirit of DIY, you can easily substitute some materials for other items you may have on hand instead of the ones listed. Better yet, use the ones here as inspiration and make your own bigger, better version!

Inside, you'll find grappling hooks, trebuchets, darts and more—all made out of office supplies! We've even included some fun non-warfare projects at the end to keep you entertained in times of peace.

—Mike Warren (mikeasaurus)

Editor's Note

The wonderful thing about Instructables is that they come in all shapes and sizes. Some users include hundreds of high-quality pictures and detailed instructions with their projects; others take the minimalist approach and aim to inspire similar ideas than to facilitate carbon copies.

One of the biggest questions we faced when putting this book together was: How do we convey the sheer volume of ideas in the finite space of a book?

As a result, if you're already familiar with some of the projects in this book, you'll notice that selected photos made the jump from the computer screen to the printed page. Similarly, when dealing with extensive electronic coding or complex science, we suggest that anyone ready to start a project like that visit the Instructables' online page, where you often find lots more images, links, multimedia attachments, and downloadable material to help you along the way. This way, if you get stuck on a particular step or want more reading on a project, more information is just a click away.

*Special thanks to Instructables Interactive Designer Gary Lu for the Instructables Robot illustrations!

Section 1

Bows and Arrows

The bow and arrow was probably prehistoric man's first advanced weapon—knowing that there are only so many foes that can be defeated by a club, a more sophisticated approach was needed. The bow and arrow is where we start our office weaponry; a classic ranged weapon that's silent and accurate.

Making your own bow and arrow out of odds and ends around your cubicle is an easy way to get your feet wet in the world of office warfare. There are simple designs to start with, moving up to more technical types of arrow slingers, for those with loads of time between meetings that really want to build something special. Get ready to nock an arrow and fire! Your coworkers won't know what hit them.

Popsicle Stick Crossbow

By pmac93
(http://www.instructables.com/
id/Popsicle-Stick-Crossbow-2/)

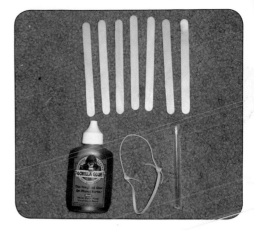

Okay, here's my made up version of a crossbow. It's kind of like a BIC pen crossbow on a larger scale. I used gorilla glue on all of the joints of the body, but hot glue would probably work.

Step 1: Materials

- 7 popsicle sticks
- Pen tube (pen minus the writing part and end cap)
- Chip clip or some other strong clip (not a clothes pin)
- Gorilla glue or hot glue
- Bamboo skewers for ammo

Step 2: Make the Body

Start by gluing a popsicle stick perpendicular to two others, as shown in the first picture. Then glue another one down the middle of the two parallel sticks, like the picture. I used other popsicle sticks to support it. Then, glue two more just like the front half of the body, but without the cross piece. Make a notch in each end of the cross piece.

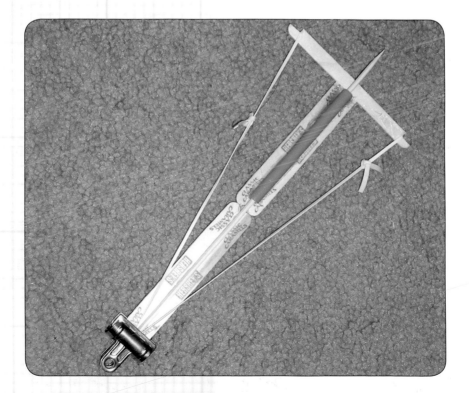

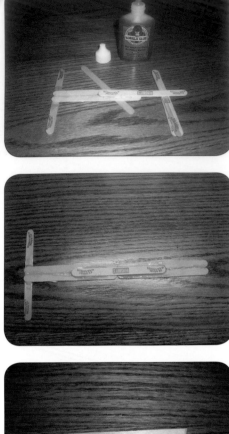

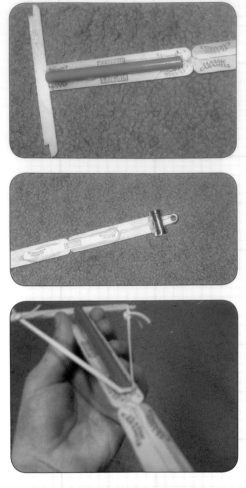

Step 3: Add the Pen Tube and Clip

Glue the pen tube in the center of the front half of the body. This will guide the arrow as it goes out. Now just clip the clip onto the end of the whole thing and put some glue on it so it only opens to the top. Add the rubber band as shown, wrapping it around the notches and onto the end of the pen. It is helpful to put a notch in the end of the pen so the rubber band doesn't slip off and to help load it.

Step 4: Load and Fire

Shove a bamboo skewer in the pen tube and center it on the rubber band so it stays. Push it all the way in, center it on the body, and clip it. It improves the flight and makes it easier to load if you add a little bit of electrical tape on the front of a skewer. Fire by just unclipping the arrow.

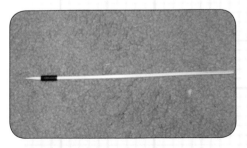

Simple Bottle Cap Crossbow

By tankguy
(http://www.instructables.com/
id/Simple-Bottle-Cap-Crossbow/)

In this Instructable, I'll show you how to make an easy, simple crossbow from a recycled bottle cap in under 5 minutes. Enjoy, and be safe.

Step 1: Materials
Supplies
- 1 Bottle Cap
- 2 Toothpicks
- 1 Rubber Band
- Tape

Tools
- Scissors
- Swiss Army Knife

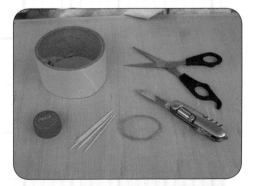

Step 2: Holes . . .

First you'll need to make four holes in the bottle cap, like in the picture. Think of it as two sets of holes that are *exactly* opposite each other.

To make the holes, I used the can opener on my knife, which has a very sharp point. I then expanded the hole by forcing my screwdriver through it.

Note: Make sure one set of holes is slightly lower than the other so that the toothpicks don't touch each other.

Step 3: Toothpick

Now put one toothpick through a set of holes and firmly secure with tape. This toothpick will act as the anchor for the rubber band we attach in the next step.

5

Step 5: Ammunition

In order to prepare your toothpick ammo for firing, cut off one of the pointy ends with your scissors. This will allow for better grip when firing.

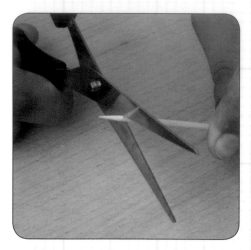

Step 4: Rubber Band

Now secure the rubber band around the toothpick with a Lark's head hitch. I tried my best to show it with pictures.

Step 6: Loading & Firing

To load the crossbow, take your ammunition and thread it through the remaining holes. Now pull it back with the rubber band and fire away.

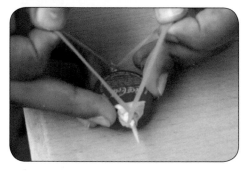

Step 7: Now What?

Well, there you have it, a pocket sized tooth pick shooting cross bow. You can use your shiny new weapon to annoy people at school, work, or anywhere else you might find yourself.

Hidden Crossbow

By DucttapeNinja
(http://www.instructables
.com/id/Hidden-Crossbow-
version-20/)

A while back, I found instructions for a clever office supply bow and arrow and was inspired. I decided to step things up a notch. In the end, I had a nifty little "crossbow" that straps to the inner arm, perfectly concealed by a loose sleeve. With just a flick of the wrist, your classmates won't know what hit them!

This is the second incarnation of the design. The first was held together entirely with gorilla tape and I only had enough pictures for a slide show.

Careful! Though not as powerful as other designs, this thing can still do some damage. Do not point it toward the face; it could easily take out an eye. Do not aim anywhere that can potentially damage something. It's awkward aiming with the forearm, so its accuracy can be a hit or miss (pun intended).

Step 1: You Will Need

Materials
- At least three BIC ballpoint pens
- A thin rubber band*
- A clothespin*
- Several craft (popsicle) sticks
- A length of strong thread*
- Duct tape (No project is complete without it!)
- A ring (optional)

*Take care selecting these items. Too strong a rubber band can't be held back by the clothespin. Too strong a clothespin will break your thread. If everything is too strong, you risk yanking the whole thing off your arm when you go to fire.

Tools

I was able to rig one of these with mostly scissors and a roll of gorilla tape in the back of class, so don't sweat the details. However, I have found these to work quite well:
- Scissors
- A hot glue gun
- A small-bit drill
- A fine tooth saw
- Duct tape (So important it deserves to be named twice.)

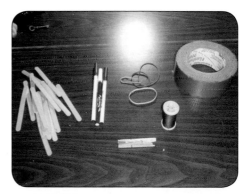

7

Step 2: All Your Base

The base of this rig is made out of craft sticks. I used seven, but the exact number can vary if you wish. I suggest keeping it about the width of the wrist to prevent it from shifting around.

What is important is that you make sure you use an odd number of craft sticks. While most of the sticks are flush, the middle one is pulled back about 1⅛ inches. (All my measurements are arbitrary and based on how things fit together. Your measurements may vary.) This is where you will attach your clothespin.

Bind the sticks together tightly with tape. You may want to push it down onto your arm afterward to get it to contour to your wrist.

Step 3: The Pen is Mightier

Now it's time to take apart those pens. They should come apart easily with a little effort. Apart from the cap, these pens are made out of four parts with names I am about to make up: the nose piece, the ink cartridge, the shaft, and the end-cap.

Take one of the shafts and shave it down to a length that will fit sideways in your sleeve without making a noticeable bulge in the fabric. Mine came out to a little less than 4 inches.

Find the middle of your shortened shaft and make a hole all the way through. I was able to do this with an X-acto knife and screwdriver. If you have the tools, I'd expect a heated piece of metal to work pretty well. Make the hole wide enough for the nose piece to fit snugly inside.

Cut some notches in the ends of the shaft to hold your rubber band. Now attach the entire thing to the body of the crossbow with tape and/or any other fasteners/adhesives you are using, with the nose piece centered over the gap to the left of the uneven middle craft stick. Make sure the tapered end of the nose piece points outward.

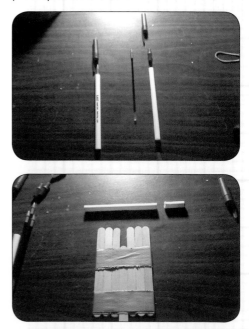

Step 4: The Guide Rail

Take the second pen shaft and split it lengthwise in two. Try to shave down the edges until they are as straight and smooth as possible. The rubber band will be flying through here and you don't want it to snag.

Take your clothespin and drill a hole through the two ends you pinch together. Position the clothespin on the body of the rig, over the craft stick that sticks out on the back end. Make sure the hole in the clothespin is far enough back so as not to be covered by the craft stick, and secure it down.

Take one half of the split shaft and shorten it to fit between the closed end of the clothespin and the nose piece centered between the crossbow arms. Glue it down.

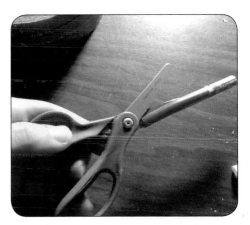

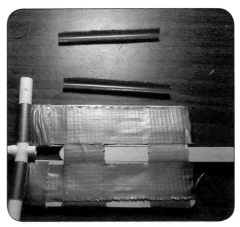

9

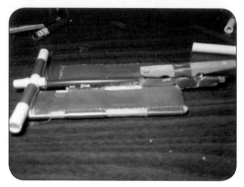

into it. Do not make another roll with the second piece. This tape creation has to bear the tension of the rubber band, so try to make it as secure as possible.

Now, time to "string your bow." The rubber band stretches around the arms, fitting into the notches you cut into the ends. The tape assembly should sit in the guide groove made from the half-pen shaft. The rolled end should fit in the clothespin when pulled back.

If everything is in order, go ahead and tape the other half of that pen shaft over it. Make sure to only use tape here, as it attaches to moving parts and must flex accordingly. Anchor one end of the shaft to the top of the clothespin and the other end to the crossbow arms. You may have to glue in something to raise the top half of the groove up high enough that it doesn't slow down firing.

By now it's suitable as an office crossbow. Now on to the part that makes it unique.

Step 5: "Twang!"

Now comes the tricky part. Here is where you construct a special fitting for your rubber band that fits into the catch (the clothespin):

1. Take a thin strip of duct tape and roll it up part way. Roll with the sticky side in.
2. Place one of your end caps on the edge of the unrolled end, on the sticky side. This part will hold the bolt (ink cartridge) and keep it from falling off the rubber band. Place the rubber band just behind the end cap.
3. Cut partway in on the strip of tape on each side, behind the rubber band and before the roll. Fold these new tabs into the sticky area between them. Press what's left up the sides of the end cap. To be safe, you will want to secure the other side of the end cap with a shorter piece of tape with similar tabs cut

through the hole on the bottom side that leads to the half shaft you just glued in. If your thread isn't strong enough to pull the two ends together you may want to double it up. After the clothespin, string the thread through the half shaft on the underside of the rig. An easy way of doing this is threading a sewing needle and dropping it through. Tie the open end to a ring or into a loop.

Now it's time to add the straps. I made mine out of strips of tape, layered sticky-side in, fastened around my arm with more strips of tape. I made them kind of hastily to illustrate.

For ammunition, take the ink cartridges and cut them down to size. You want the back end to sit in the cup of the tape assembly when pulled back and the point to fit closely to the nose piece without going in.

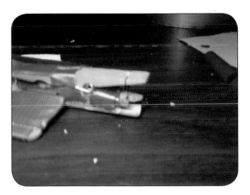

Step 6: Finishing Up

Take your remaining pen shaft and split it in two lengthwise, like the last one. Glue it to the underside of the base along the middle, right under the hole in the clothespin.

Tie your thread to the outside arm of the clothespin before stringing it

Step 7: Annoy the Heck Out of Your Friends and Coworkers

Now, time to strap the whole thing to your arm and try it out. Keep the ring-on-a-string on a short enough leash that it pulls open the clothespin when you bend your wrist back. Put it on your finger. Pull the tape assembly back into the catch (clothespin) and load in one of your bolts (shortened ink cartridge). Now you're ready to put tiny dimples in something!

Make sure it is strapped to your inner arm if you want to hide it in your sleeve, that way gravity will pull it open, allowing your shot clearance. What this contraption lacks in strength it makes up with in the whole "What the #&@% was that!?" factor.

Bonus Features

For added strength, you can wind the free end of the rubber band around the nose piece.

Should the string break, you have a fail-safe. Push in the back of the clothespin with your free hand. (You'll want to know where that is anyway, it's easy to bump it on something and shoot yourself in the hand.)

Push the ink cartridge slightly into the nose piece (that's where it was made to fit). Now it won't fall out when you point your arm down. Make sure not to press it in too far, or when you go to shoot, it won't budge.

Add a safety by lengthening the string so it will only fire when the ring is on the second knuckle of your finger. Now when the ring is all the way down on your finger, you don't have to worry about accidentally shooting yourself in the chin when you try to pick your nose. When you want to get ready to fire, just discreetly push the ring up to the middle of your finger.

Now just get creative! Add a place to hold extra bolts. Find a way to improve it (shouldn't be too hard). Personally, I've always wanted to see one of these rigged as a trap inside someone's desk drawer.

Reception Desk Paperclip Crossbow

By samaside
(http://www.instructables.com/
id/Reception-Desk-Paperclip-
Crossbow/)

Like most people these days and in this economy, I had two jobs back in 2011. One was working with kids doing all kinds of fun projects and the other was working nights and weekends at a reception desk, filing things away. I actually like both. There's something simple and calming about just putting files away.

Anyway, my last night at work was pretty slow and I was feeling a bit bored. Everyone knows what it feels like as you edge closer and closer to your last day at work. You just stop focusing and look for anything to grab your attention. For whatever reason, I got it in my head that I was going to try and make a crossbow out of the office supplies I had handy. I blame Instructables—I had been browsing through various little office weapon guides to waste time, and I got it into my head that I wanted to try and make something super simple that anyone could with handy office supplies.

Thus, after about forty five minutes of abject boredom and some awful 90s movie on the television in the lobby, the paperclip crossbow was born.

Step 1: The Supplies

Now, the supplies you will need are fairly simple.
- One rubber band
- Four paperclips
- Thumb tacks

Additionally, you may choose to have scotch tape or duct tape on hand for an optional step later.

For paperclips, I like to use two long and two short, but you can use four paperclips of the same length as well.

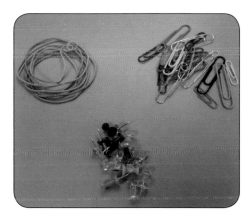

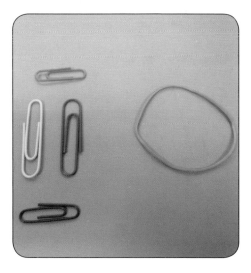

Step 2

First, we're going to shape the front part of the crossbow. Take a paperclip—in this case a small one—and bend it out straight. You can leave the little hook

13

end curved if you like because you'll basically just be making a smaller curve on the other end to make it match. It's a fairly simple step. Just follow along with the pictures!

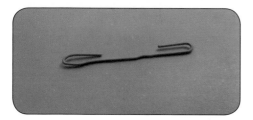

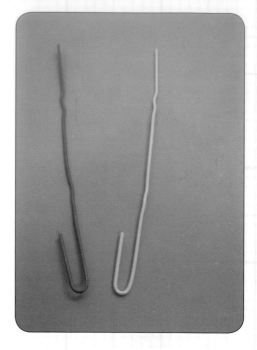

Step 3

Now, take the two longer paperclips or the two paperclips you are going to use for the shaft of the crossbow. Do the same thing as in step one—straighten them out, except for the smaller hooked end. Do not, however, make a hook on the other end of these two paperclips. Again, see the pictures.

Step 4

This is where it starts to get complicated.

You will need all three of the paperclips we have used so far. You're going to take the longer paperclips and place the end that does not have a hook up against the front-piece paperclip. See the pictures for a better illustration. You will then wrap both of them very tightly around that front piece.

You want to leave a little gap between the two paperclips to create a little cradle or groove for the paperclip you will launch. It needs to be fairly small, just big enough to keep the paperclip vaguely in place.

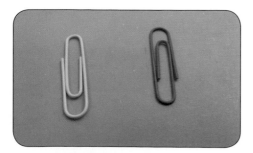

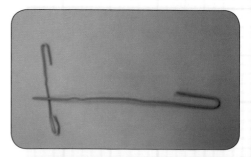

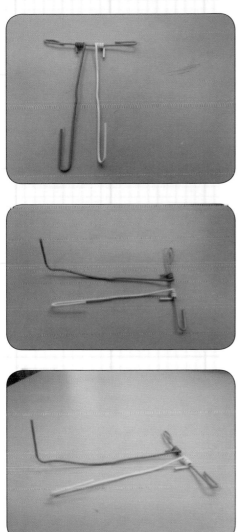

The pictures show you how I managed to get them together.

The key here is to make the twists tight so the grip is solid and does not move, twist, or slide around.

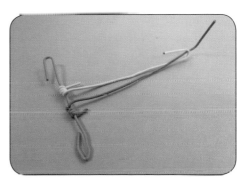

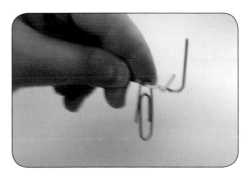

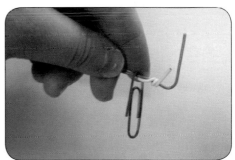

Step 5

This is probably the most complicated step and the hardest step to explain. This is because there's not really a right way to do this. You basically need to take the other small paperclip and the ends of the two longer ones and make a grip for your crossbow. You can do this in various ways. I chose to straighten the end of one of the long ones and hook it in the bent end of the other. Then I took the small paperclip, slipped those ends into the center of it, and sort of twisted it all together.

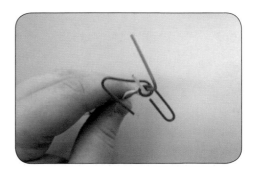

Step 6

You'll need the rubber band now. The length doesn't particularly matter. Smaller is better; obviously you can't use a big one like I used in my desktop catapult. Play around with the rubber bands you have handy and you'll find one that works best for you. I used rubber bands of various types. You'll want it to be a thin one, though. I doubt the thicker ones would work. (I can't say for certain because I never tried them, but I highly doubt it.)

So, take the rubber band and place it in the hooked ends of the front piece. Twist the paperclip ends around the rubber band to keep it in place, as seen in the pictures.

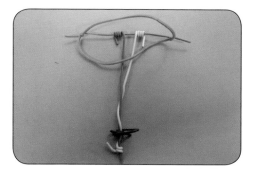

Step 7: (Optional)

Hurray! Technically, your crossbow is completed. It will work as it is.

This is the first optional part of the crossbow design. You might have noticed it back in Step 6. I chose to take part of one of the longer paperclips making up the shaft and bend it upward.

That way, I could rest the paperclip on it and keep it permanently primed to fire. It's a fairly simple adjustment to make, even if you've already twisted your paperclips together. It just needs to be a little piece to hook the rubber band on to keep it primed.

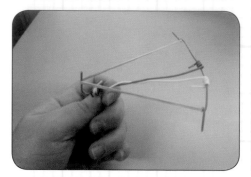

Step 8: (Optional)

You can take a piece of tape and add it to the back of the rubber band to keep it together. It also makes it a lot easier for the rubber band to fully hit the thumb tack that you place in the groove. It will work without the tape and, while I used duct tape here, you can honestly use any sort of tape for this step.

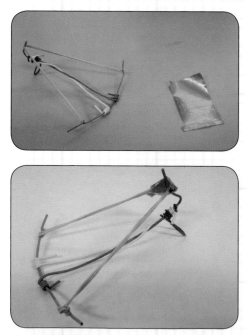

Step 9: Ready, Aim, Fire!

And, believe it or not, you're done! That's it. Fairly simple, like I said. It's not the straightest shot necessarily, but it's fairly fast. We actually got it to stick into a cork board when firing from six feet away. It depends a lot on the size of the rubber band and how much slack you have. So give it a shot. (Pardon the pun.) See how yours works. And make adjustments as necessary.

Step 10: Variations

I made a few of these as I was perfecting the design and creating the step-by-step pictures.

In my trails, I found that different materials used to make the crossbow do sort of matter. The more traditional, silver paperclips are a bit stronger than the prettier, colored, plastic-covered paperclips. The plastic-covered ones tended to bend a bit easier. That was the only real difference. Well, that and the fact that the traditional silver ones tended to hurt you a bit more when you fingers slipped and snagged on the edges.

Best of luck in creating your own crossbows and variations of the design!

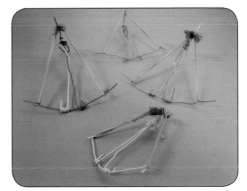

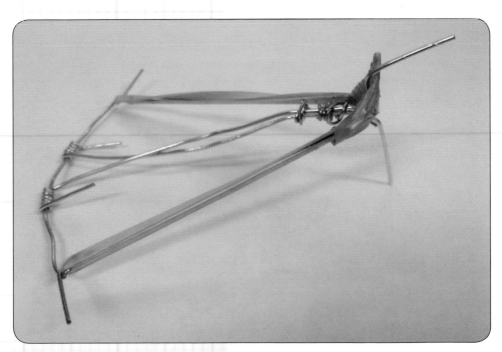

bows and arrows

Arrows for Paperclip Bow

By archer0382
(http://www.instructables.com/
id/arrows-for-paper-clip-bow/)

Need good target arrows for paperclip bow? Well, these work great. They are accurate and can stick in wood. Warning: These can puncture skin; do not shoot at any living thing.

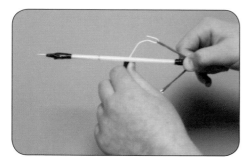

Step 1: Supplies needed

- Paperclip bow
- Straws
- Tape (eletrical or duck tape works best)
- Toothpicks
- Scissors
- Paper to make your own targets (I use paper frogs, as shown in the picture below.)
- Markers for decoration (optional)

Step 2: Preparing Straws

You only need to do this step if you are using bendy straws. Cut under the bendy part of the straw and keep the long end. These will be the arrow shafts.

Step 3: Putting the Points on the Arrows

Take the piece of straw and wrap some tape around one end of it. Ffter you have wrapped the tape a couple times around one end, make sure there is a hole big enough to stick the toothpick in. Stick the toothpick in halfway and squeeze the tape around it so it will stay. This picture is of the tape wrapped around the arrow without the tip.

Step 4: Making the Nocks

Cut a little ways down the opposite side 2 times. Make the cuts across from each other and put a piece of tape around the bottom of the cut so it doesn't split the straw.

Step 5: Aim and Fire

Take your bow and arrow and knock it on the rubber band. Pull back, aim, and fire.

Clear BIC Pen Bow and Arrow

By EPL
http://www.instructables.com/
id/Bic-pen--bow-%26-arrow/

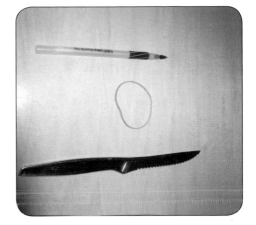

This is a bow and arrow made of a clear BIC pen (similar to the regular BIC pen bow and arrow created by postapoc with a few moderations that could possibly make it better).

Step 2: Pen
Now, take apart the BIC pen.

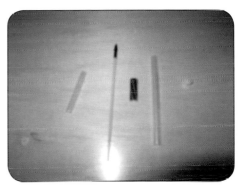

Step 1: Materials
The materials are a BIC Round Stic Grip Ultra Ball Pen, a rubber band, and a knife.

Step 3: The Hole
Using the knife, make a hole in the pen big enough to fit the grip. Be careful

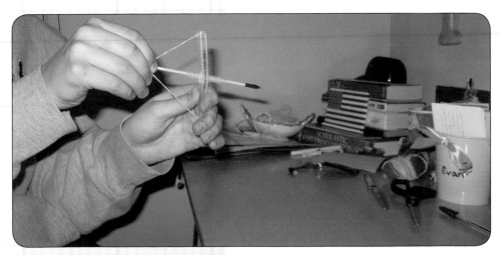

not to make it too big or else you will break the pen.

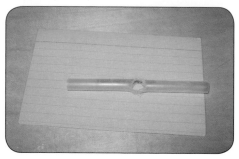

Step 4: Grip or Long Thing

Put the pen grip into the hole that you just made. You can also use the long thing that was used in the other bow and arrow, but the grip is better with the pen grip because it is shorter and wider. Shortness is good because the ammo will get to the rubber band quickly, which means more power. Wideness is good because you can use a lot different ammunitions.

Step 5: Rubber Band

Cut 2 notches at the top and bottom of the pen to hold the rubber band in place. Once you have cut these, slide the rubber bands in place.

Step 6: Launch

Put your ammo (the ink canister works very well) through the grip or long thing to the rubber band. Then pull back the rubber band with the ammo to your desired power and let go.

How to Make a Mini Wooden Crossbow

By swisel
(http://www.instructables.com/
id/how-to-make-a-mini-wooden-
crossbow/)

In this Instructable i will be showing you how to make a powerful, small wooden crossbow out of spare parts that should not be too hard to find.

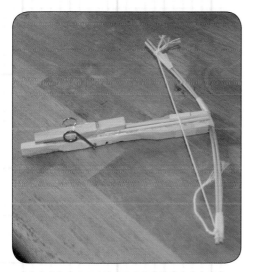

Step 1:
You will need:
- Two pieces of wood, 17 cm × 1 cm
- Wooden clothespin
- Hot glue gun
- Knife
- Glue sticks
- Masking tape
- Electrical tape
- 4 wooden skewers
- Scissors
- Some kind of small saw
- Snippers
- Thread or wire

Step 2: The bow
Take two of your skewers and cut off the sharp tips. Tape them together about 1 cm from the ends. Now, tie your wire to one end, bend it and tie it to the other end.

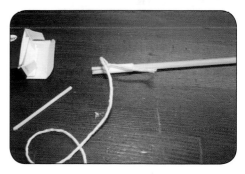

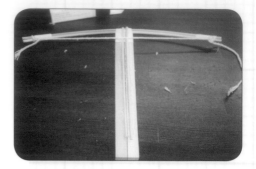

Step 3: The body

Hot glue your two pieces of wood together. Glue and tape your bow on the body.

Step 4: Arrow supports

Pick up those last two skewers. Cut them down to about the same length as the body, maybe a little shorter. Try to glue them close to each other without touching.

Step 5: The trigger

Pick up your wooden clothespin and drag the bottom off. We only need the part with the steel coil. Cut off as much as you can from both sides (but no more than I did, please see pictures). This will let us put on the trigger). Then make a groove 6.5cm from the back end and 0.5 cm deep. Clip on the clothespin.

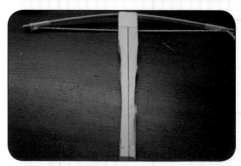

22

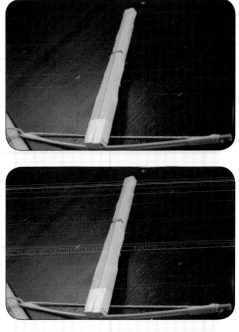

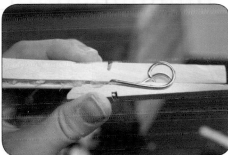

arrow and then cut to the shape shown in the picture.

Step 7: Finishing up

Now have fun and remember to be careful. NEVER point it at anything living!!!! This is extremely powerful! It is a fun toy to bring to work or school. You can even bring it in your pocket; just conceal it with your t-shirt.

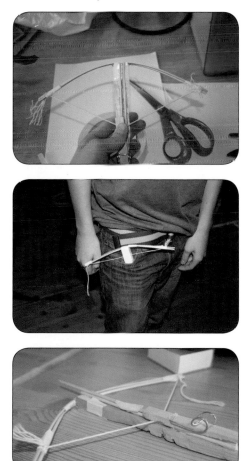

Step 6: Arrow

It's your choice now; you can make your arrow out of almost anything. I made mine out of a skewer. You can use the rest of the arrow holder. Just put some masking tape on the back of the

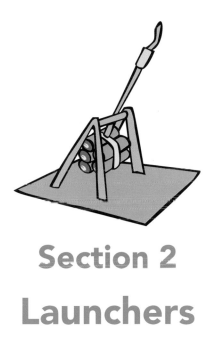

Section 2

Launchers

- **The Viking Catapult**
- **Mini Catapult from Office/School Supplies**
- **Fingernail Clipper Catapult**
- **Youth Center Desktop Slingshot Catapult**
- **The Office Supplies Trebuchet**
- **Liquid Fuel Rocket**
- **Pocket Slingshot**

Since the dawn of time, siege-engines have been one of the most effective weapons. The desktop version hasn't been around as long, but no matter the size the concept remains the same, and so do the results. Launchers can be any type of mechanism that hurls a projectile towards your enemy while you are safely hidden behind your cubicle fortifications, perfect for that long-range assault. Whether you prefer a tried and tested approach like a spring loaded catapult or counterweight trebuchet, or a more modern approach like a liquid-fueled rocket, there's a desktop siege-engine here that you can build with things lying around your workspace.

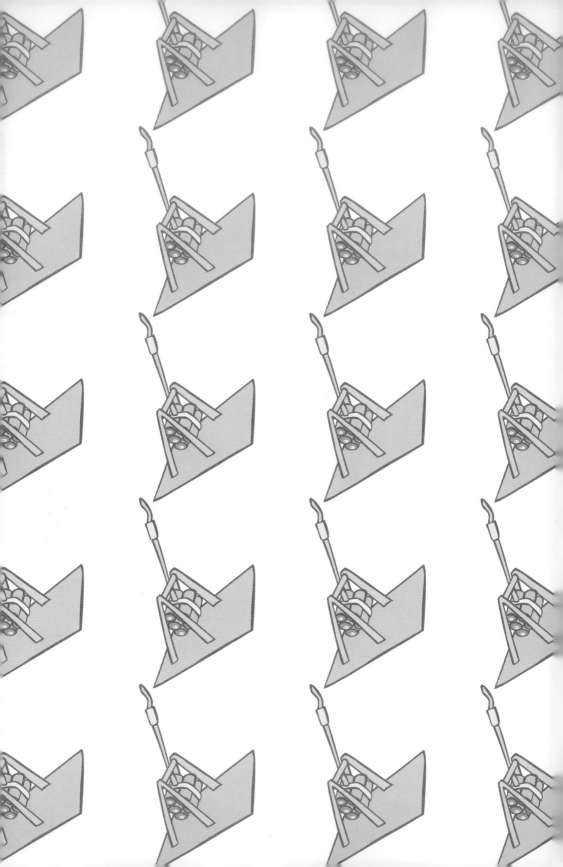

The Viking Catapult
By M3G
(http://www.instructables.com/
id/The-Viking-Catapult/)

This should teach your co-workers who's boss. Spend half an hour making it, then have hours of fun hassling your co-workers or target shooting. Mine shot a pencil eraser about 30 feet easily.

Step 1: What You Need

- 5 pencils
- 2 pens
- A plastic bottle cap
- At least 14 elastics
- A craft knife or pair of scissors

Step 2: Making the Frame Part 1

Take three pencils, arrange them in a triangle, and use elastics to hold them together. This will be the base. Use an elastic to attach another two pencils together into a V shape. Then take the V shape and use elastics to attach the forks to two of the corners of the triangle.

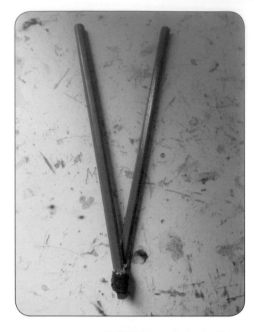

Step 3: Making the Frame Part 2

Place an elastic over one of the arms on the V and pull it through itself (see the first picture). Put the pen through the elastic, as shown in the second picture. Pull the elastic tight and wrap it around the pen and frame. Repeat this for the other side. Do the same thing with the other end of the pens near the back of the frame.

Step 4: The Ammo Pouch

Use the craft knife to cut one hole in the top of the plastic bottle cap and three holes in the sides, roughly equal distances apart. Thread elastics through the holes in the sides and pull them through themselves to secure them. Tie a knot in another elastic and thread it through the hole in the top of the cap, with the knot inside the cap. Make sure the knot doesn't come through the cap when you pull the elastic.

Step 5: Bringing It All Together

Attach the pouch to the bottom of the frame the same way you attached the elastics to the sides of the bottle cap. Loop two of the elastics over the pens. You can repeat these steps to increase power. To fire, place your ammo in the bottle cap and pull back on the elastic protruding from the back of the cap, then release.

Mini Catapult from Office/ School Supplies

By epic chicken ninja
(http://www.instructables
.com/id/mini-catapult-from-
officeschool-suplies/)

Is the boy at the front of the class always annoying you? Is your colleague always distracting you? If so, then follow these 4 easy steps to build a mini catapult.

Step 1: What You Need
- Bulldog clip
- Rubber band
- Ink cartridge or pencil

Step 2: Wrap Around
Wrap the rubber band around the handles of the bulldog clip. Double it over if your band is too long.

Step 3: Nearly There
Place the ink cartridge (or pencil) in between the body of the clip and the handle.

Step 4: Now for Revenge!
To fire the catapult, just hold down the handle, which has nothing between it and the body of the clip, onto the table. Then, pull back the other handle, add some ammo, and release the handle that has the ammo on it.

Fingernail Clipper Catapult

By Geek Gecko
(http://www.instructables.com/
id/Fingernail-Clipper-Catapult/)

In this Instructable, I will show you how to make a catapult out of nothing more than a fingernail and or toenail clippers, along with some other easily accessible materials.

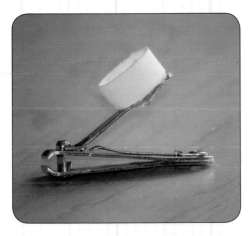

Step 1: Materials and Tools

- A hot glue gun
- Fingernail clippers
- A water bottle cap

Step 2: Assembling

All you need to do is simply hot glue the cap onto the top of the fingernail clippers, leaving a small amount of room on the top to put your finger.

Step 3: Firing

Simply push down on the fingernail clippers and release. Some objects that you might want to fire are paper wads, BB's, beads, and other miscellaneous small items.

WARNING: Do *not* fire at other people or animals without their consent. Even then, don't fire near the face! I am not responsible if you hurt somebody or lose a pet!

Youth Center Desktop Slingshot Catapult

By samaside
(http://www.instructables
.com/id/Youth-Center-Desktop-
Slingshot-Catapult/)

Originally this design was created for in-house use only. I work as a tech lab program lead for a youth center on the army base where I grew up. I teach science and technology and do assorted projects with middle school and high school students. When I first got started at the center, I missed the deadline for requesting materials and such, so I had to be a little creative for those first few weeks. This was one of the projects I came up with on the fly.

I knew that I wanted to do a series of catapults with the kids, but we didn't have the supplies on hand for the more advanced designs. This project was the result of a day's worth of trial and error. The only supplies I used were the ones I had on hand, and even the rubber bands I used had to be scrounged up from other programs' supplies. I was surprised at how well it worked and the kids loved them.

The pictures I took here were originally intended for future tech lab folks since I am about to leave my job to go to law school down in Arizona. But we've recently gotten a lot of new kids in the program who have been interested in making the catapults. So I decided to go ahead and post this tutorial for them and for anyone else who might be interested in putting the spare office supplies they've got lying around to good use.

So far we have successfully run the program with my older kids as well as the elementary age kids at one of our other centers. It takes about fifteen to twenty minutes for me to make one and about forty-ish minutes for the kids. (And if a project can keep a middle schooler's attention for that long, you know it has to be good!) It takes longer depending on the size of the group, too.

Okay, on with the instructable!

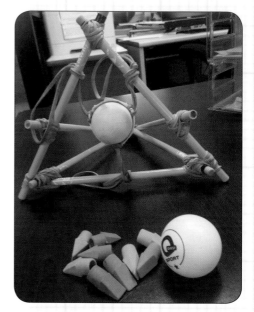

Step 1: The Supplies

As I mentioned earlier, the supplies I used were just random things I could collect around the center. Customized pencils were in abundance, and I was able to collect enough rubber bands to piece it all together. The only thing that needed to be bought for the project was the rubber bands since I had used the few we had on the prototypes.

You will need
- 12+ rubber bands (three of which must be the same type)
- Duct tape for making the pouch
- 7 pencils
- Scissors
- Ammo

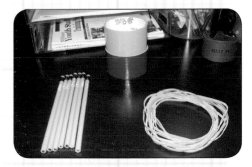

Step 2: The Base

The first part of making this slingshot catapult is the base. It's fairly simple; all you need to do is make a triangle out of the pencils.

You need to take

• Three pencils
• Three rubber bands

You will take two of the pencils and use the rubber band to bind them together. A crisscross sort of pattern works best. Wrap the rubber band tightly so the pencils don't slip. You will then repeat this step twice more to bind all three pencils together in a triangle shape. You will want to make a sort of cross bar at the front of the catapult, so make sure to appoint one pencil as the "front pencil." You will want to make sure you bind the other two either on top of it or below it. It doesn't really matter if you put them on top or on bottom of that front pencil. Nor does it matter which of the pencils is on top when you bind the two support pencils together to finish the triangle.

Once you have successfully made the triangle, you can move on to the next step.

Step 3: The Frame—Part 1

The next step is to create the first part of the full frame for firing.

You will need

• Two pencils
• Three rubber bands

First, you need to take one of the pencils and place the end of it between the two ends of the pencils on one side of the front of your base. You will then take a rubber band and wrap it around this new pencil, as well as around the other two. If you have a limited number of rubber bands or did not wrap the

33

pencils on your base together tight enough, you can instead pull the rubber band and squeeze the third pencil end in with the other two ends.

Repeat this step again with the second pencil and the other side of the front of the base. See the pictures for reference.

Once you have done this you will bring the two pencils together at the top and bind them together with another rubber band.

Step 4: The Frame—Part 2

The next part of the frame will provide support for the firing section.

You will need

- Two additional pencils
- 3–4 rubber bands

This part was complicated for the kids but is not as hard as it may seem. All you need to do is take one of the pencils and tie the end close to the bottom of one of the pencils making up the front part of the frame. It needs to be down low to offer support but also not get in the way of where the firing pouch will be tied.

You will then take the other pencil and bind it to the other side. Make sure you bind it to the outside and not the inside or you will limit your firing space.

When both support pencils are bound to the front of the frame, take one to two more rubber bands and bind them in the back to the back cross-section of the triangular base.

None of the other materials I tried worked as well.

You will need

- Duct tape
- Scissors
- 3 rubber bands

What you need to do is cut or tear a strip of duct tape. The bigger you want the pouch, the bigger your strip should be. It should probably be around six inches maximum. Maybe closer to four. I've never really measured it to be honest. You'll take the piece of tape and sort of wrap it in on itself. Once you have a sort of cup, you'll fill the interior with other strips of duct tape so the inside is no longer sticky.

Once the pouch is made, you will need to cut three holes in the pouch near the edges. There should be as equal a distance between the three holes as possible.

You will then take your rubber hands and loop them through the holes. Pull them tight.

After you have gotten all three rubber bands secured through their respective holes, you will take a few strips of additional duct tape and wrap them around the knots. This will keep them in place and also keep the rubber bands from ripping through the loop holes with excessive use.

Once your pouch is ready, you can tie it to the frame as shown in the final picture.

Step 5: The Pouch

There are a lot of different ways to make the pouch. When I was coming up with the design, I made it out of duct tape because that was what I had on hand. But I suppose you could make it out of other stuff you have on hand.

Step 6: The Ammo

Your catapult can effectively launch anything small enough to fit into the pouch. The original design shot rubber eraser ends but they tended to get lost too easily behind the computer desks in my lab. So when I made them with the kids, we used some old ping pong balls.

The kids, of course, wanted to use thumb tacks and rocks. If you are doing this with kids, you need to set ground rules early.

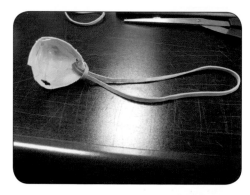

Step 7: The Finished Product!

Obviously, the design is fairly simple. There are a lot of ways to change it up and innovate. Once the kids got the hang of the basic design, they went crazy and came up with all kinds of other little ways to tweak their catapults. I included a couple of pictures of the catapults we made as a group.

The Office Supplies Trebuchet

By Scissorman
(http://www.instructables
.com/id/The-Office-supplies-
trebuchet/)

Bored at work? Build your own 3in trebuchet out of paperclips and throw balls of blu-tac up to an amazing 4 feet. *Wow!* Please excuse the number of steps. It is really easy and can be made within an hour from bits lying around the office (hence very cheaply).

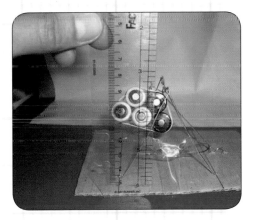

Step 1: The Tools and Materials List

- 1 pair of pliers (needle nose would be best, where available)
- 1 pair of scissors (yay for scissors)
- 8 paperclips
- Cellotape
- Thin string/thread
- Blu-tac
- Corrugated card (approximately 6in × 6in)
- Ballast (I used a bunch of batteries from our recycling box)
- Rubber band

Step 2: Straightening the Paperclips

Use the pliers to make the paperclips as straight as possible.

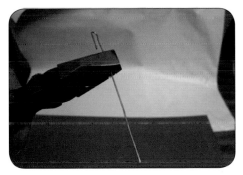

Step 3: Now Shape Them

At the very end of four of the paperclips, make an eyelet big enough to insert an ex paperclip through (but not much bigger). At the other end, make a dog leg. Bend approximately ½ inch of the non-eyeleted end at right angles (90 degrees) to the eyelet. All will become clear very soon.

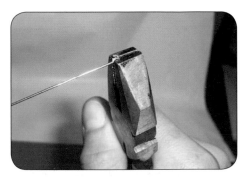

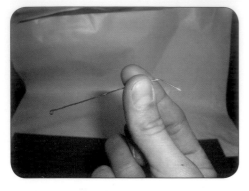

Step 4: The Axle

Next, shape the axle. Make it so that the distance between the hooked ends is about two inches. It should be wider than your intended ballast. The V shape (U shape in this case; needle-nose pliers are best for this sort of thing) must be centered on the axle.

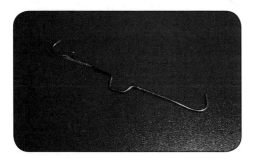

Step 5: The Arm

Make a loop in another paperclip about ½ inch from the end. At the same end, make another eyelet. Make a small hook at the other end.

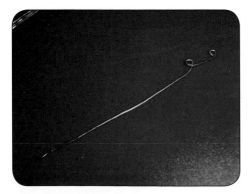

Step 6: The Trigger

This step is a little hard to describe. Just look at the picture. The bump on the left is to pull. The loop on the right is there to catch the little hook on the arm. Check out the picture to see the adjustment I made to the firing mechanism in the final step. It works so much better.

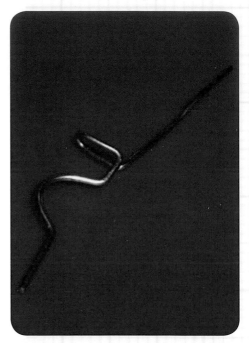

Step 7: The Components

Here's what you should have so far.

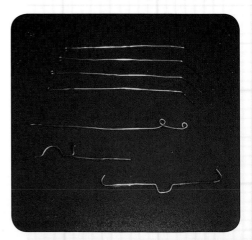

launchers

Step 8: Assembling the Parts

Take the axle and insert it through the loop in the arm (not the eyelet) so that it sits in the V. I wrapped Cello Tape around the axle on either side of the V just to give it some thickness (so it doesn't slide all over the place).

Step 9: The Base—Part 1

Mark the base with a center line. The two lines are about 3 inches apart and the little Xs on those lines are also 3 inches apart. Cut the card to 3in × 6in pieces with the grain of the corrugation laying along the 3in distance. Mark the center line along the 6in distance and two lines 3 inches apart at right angles to the center line.

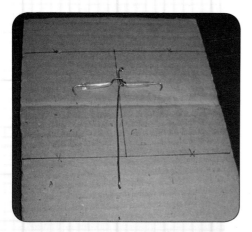

Step 10: The Base—Part 2

Poke the dog leg ends of the supports into the four Xs so that the ends are between the layers of the corrugated card. If you made the dog legs at the correct angle, they should sit as nicely as mine. Note: The new style supports from Step 3 don't get pushed through the card as shown here. Instead, insert them into the raw edge of the card. You don't have to worry about the angles of the doglegs being incorrect, and these will be much easier to secure in position with Cello Tape.

Step 11: Mounting the Axle

This is a little bit fiddly, but poke the hook ends of the axle through the eyelets in the supports, then bend the hooks down with the pliers. After that, tape between the legs to make an A-frame and then tape them to the sides of the base to prevent side to side motion.

launchers

Step 12: Mounting the Trigger

Push the end of the trigger into the layers of card where the center line intersects the support line (the side that the arm hook is on). The other end of the trigger needs to run in a slit so that it can slide back and forth. Don't make the slit too long or else you risk the trigger being pulled out. See the last step for attaching the improved version.

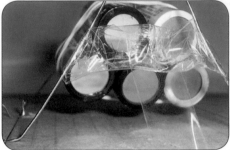

Step 13: The Ballast

Make a little hook and tape to one of the batteries. Use the rubber band to attach a whole bunch more batteries around the one with the hook. When they're all assembled and hooked on the arm, make sure the ballast is not touching the base.

Step 14: The Ammo

Take the string, put a loop in it, and push the free ends into a pea sized lump of Blu-tac. Wrap it around a couple of times and then smoosh the Blu-tac into a ball. The extra string inside will allow you some length experimentation to gain maximum distance when firing. A good length is about two thirds of the distance from the hook to the axle along the arm.

Step 15: Finishing Up

Hook the ammo over the arm, pull the arm down, and trap the hook with the trigger. Position the ammo on the center line and at full extension of the string. Aim and fire by pulling the loop on the trigger towards you. CAUTION: The arm moves fast and has a sharp little hook on it. Don't use near your eyes. Also, this isn't the most accurate piece of equipment ever designed. Just because you're aiming it forward doesn't mean the Blu-tac is going that direction. Make this at your own risk. And make sure your laces are tied. And no running with scissors.

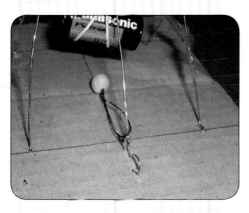

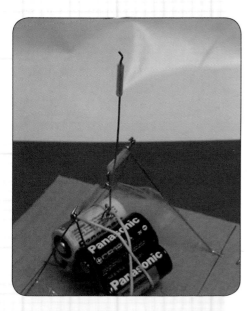

Step 16: Extras

I've already mentioned changing the string length to change the way the ammo flies. Also changing the weight of Blu-tac, changing the weight of ballast, and altering the hook angle will affect the flight path of your ammo

Step 17: Release Pin Modification

You might have already worked this out, but I found a more reliable way of launching the ammo when I was building a new one. I rotated the release pin 90 degrees so that now, instead of drawing back like a bolt, it's hinged and rolls back off the hook of the arm. You launch by pulling back on the lever. Very simple and you can use the original pin, though it may need some reshaping. Just make sure that it's placed far enough forward to release the hook and that it doesn't snag the ammo on its journey past.

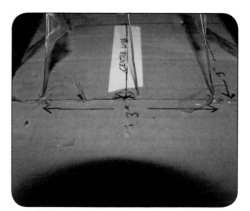

launchers

Liquid Fuel Rocket

By Tool Using Animal
(http://www.instructables.com/
id/Office-Supplies-Challenge-
Liquid-Fuel-Rocket/)

Liquid Fuel Rocket made from office supplies. Warning: this is kind of dangerous. I had one blow up in my hand already—it was more startling than anything. The two halves flew off in different directions (wear leather gloves just to be safe). But they'll fly about 75 feet straight up.

Step 1: You Will Need
- A sharpie
- Canned air
- Electrical tape (substitute packing tape)
- Ballpoint pen
- Rubber band
- Bottle cap
- Leatherman
- Robot sticker (optional)

Step 2: The Rocket Body
Disassemble the sharpie and remove the ink and the point. Cut a piece of ink tube ¾ inch long from a ballpoint pen and wrap one half with a small piece of electrical tape. Insert the tube into the

sharpie where the point used to be; tap it until firmly seated. Reassemble the two halves of the sharpie.

Step 3: Guidance

The fins are made by folding tape over on itself and attaching the tag ends to the rocket body. Trim into a rocket-ish profile. Attach three fins equally spaced around the body.

Step 4: Propulsion

Take the canned air, bend the straw down next to the body, space it out with the bottle cap, and secure with a rubber band.

Step 5: Launch

Outside, invert the can of canned air and slip the rocket body onto the straw. Hold the rocket body and depress the trigger on the can. Allow a short time to pass and release the rocket. Wash, rinse, repeat.

launchers

Pocket Slingshot

By PolishXlion
(http://www.instructables.com/
id/Pocket-Slingshot-1/)

You will need to have:
- 2 pens
- 2 rubber bands
- Scissors

Step 1: Tying up

Take a rubber band and cut it, then tie each end to one pen.

Step 2: Tie up

At the other side of the pens make the stay together by connecting them with a good rubber band.

Step 3: Shoot

To shoot pull back the cut rubber band while holding the bottom together. Use small pieces of paper or something soft.

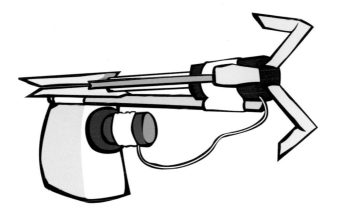

Section 3

Shooters and Darts

For the more discerning armament aficionado there are shooters and darts. The weapons in this chapter may not look that menacing, but are truly in a class of their own. Grappling hooks, marshmallow shooters, and a hand gun made form a mouse trap; these are the weapons for a true office warlord. This chapter covers some of the most technical builds we have on office supplies warfare— after you've completed a few of these the mantle will be passed onto you, to continue the time-honored tradition of misusing stationary in your workplace. Go forth, master weapons crafter, and rule your office!

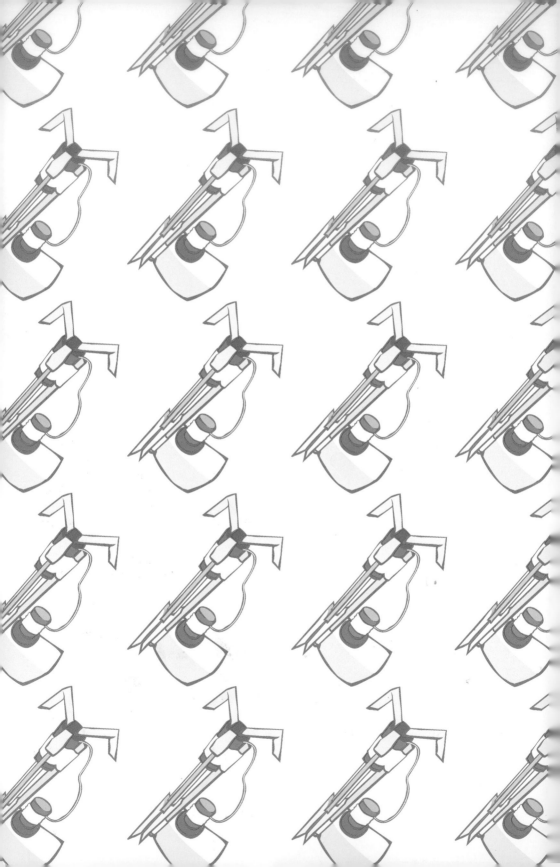

Office Supplies Grappling Gun

By Mike Warren
(mikeasaurus)
(http://www.instructables.com/
id/office-supplies-grappling-
gun/)

Ever wonder how secret agents and spies get all the cool gear? Now you can, too! Make your own mini grappling hook out of everyday office and household supplies, then let loose on a top-secret mission from Her Majesty's Secret Service.

This grappling hook design is based on the design from *Mini Weapons of Mass Destruction 2: Build a Secret Agent Arsenal* by John Austin. This book has over 30 types of weapons and gadgets that can all easily be built with office or household supplies. I chose to build a personal favorite: the grappling gun.

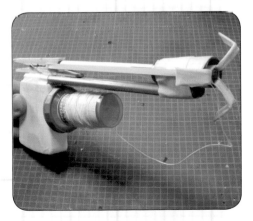

Step 1: Tools and Materials
Tools
- Masking tape
- Needle-nose pliers
- Hot glue
- Drill and bits/saw

Materials
- Floss container (full)
- 2 pencils
- Ballpoint pen (with removable back)
- Clothespin
- Cap from large marker
- Rubber band
- Pill/medicine bottle
- Paperclips

Step 2: Hooks
To make the grappling hook, start by straightening out 3 standard paperclips. Then, fold each paperclip in half and wrap them in masking tape. Using pliers, bend each wrapped paperclip into a hook-shape. (Refer to the picture for bend locations and degree.) After all 3 paperclips are bent into hooks, tape them to the ballpoint pen cap to secure them.

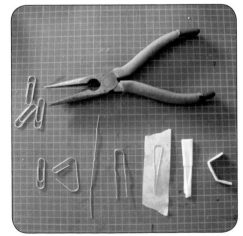

Step 3: Launch Barrel

The launch barrel is made from the cap of a large marker. Ensure that the cap you use is a larger diameter than the ballpoint pen. Create an opening in the closed end of the marker cap by either using a wide bore drill bit or simply cutting off the end of the cap. Use caution as this part can be tricky and fingers can get hurt if you're not careful.

Next, snip your rubber band and tape each end to the outside of the marker cap on opposite sides. Use plenty of tape to secure the rubber band in place. Lastly, wind a small amount of masking tape in the centre of the rubber band after it's been attached to the marker cap. This will act as the catch when you arm the grappling hook gun.

Step 4: Handle, Stock, and Trigger

Disassemble the floss container and set the spool of floss aside. Close the floss container and tape the two pencils side by side on the bottom of the floss container. This will form the handle of your grappling hook gun.

Using hot glue, stick a clothespin on top of the two pencils. This clothespin will act as the trigger.

Finally, add the launch barrel previously assembled on top of the taped-down pencils, on the opposite end from the handle, with the rubber band draw facing the clothespin.

Step 5: Spool and Line

Using the spool of floss removed from the floss container, unwind about 6m (20') of floss and tape one end to the empty pill bottle. Wind the floss around the pill bottle loosely, starting at the cap end and ending at the bottom of the bottle leaving about 30cm (1') of floss loose. Using hot glue, glue the cap of the pill bottle onto the floss container. Ensure the pill bottle is placed appropriately to allow the spool of floss to be released without catching on the underside of the barrel.

Lastly, remove the ballpoint pen bottom, feed the loose end of the floss into the back of the pen, and place the end cap back on, thereby sandwiching the floss into the back of the pen. If you're having trouble getting your floss to stay in the back of your pen, try tying a few knots in the floss and then feeding the knots into the back of the pen.

Step 6: Fire Away!

You're all done; time to test out your awesome grappling hook! Pull back the elastic band and feed the catch into the clothespin. Your grappling hook gun is now armed. Carefully feed the ballpoint pen into the barrel and place the end right up against the clothespin. Depress the clothespin to fire your grappling hook!

I managed to get mine to fire about 6m (20') after a little tweaking of the rubber band. Substituting materials may yield even more impressive results. Make sure you point this away from people, pets, plants, or anything breakable.

Have fun!

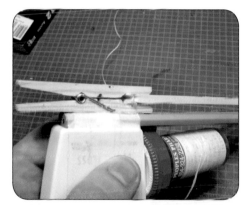

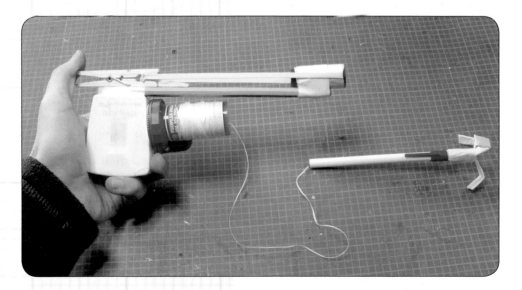

Credit Card Grappling Hook
By Noah Weinstein (noahw)
(http://www.instructables.com/
id/Credit-Card-Grappling-Hook/)

The credit card grappling hook is a whimsical little project that combines a credit card, some simple hardware, fishing line thread, and a sewing machine bobbin. It's functional for light grappling duties, but is mostly just meant to be used as a toy and for entertainment.

Step 1: Materials
The first step is to gather the materials.
- 2 credit cards
- Fishing line
- Rubber band
- Sewing machine bobbin
- Bolt
- 2 nuts
- Wing nut
- ³⁄₁₆" binding post to fit bobbin

Step 2: Attach Fishing Line to Hook
Using a larks head, attach one end of the fishing line to the grappling hook. Assemble the grappling hook so it matches the one in the photos below.

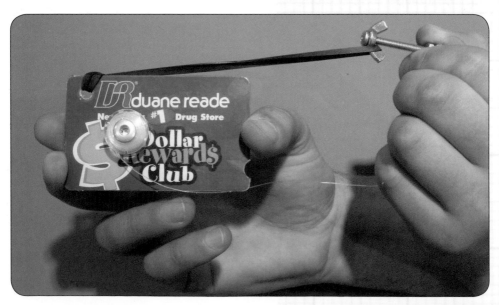

Step 3: Wind Bobbin

Wind the fishing line around the sewing bobbin just like you would wind thread on the sewing machine. This is a fast, clean, and easy way to load up your spool with many feet of grappling line.

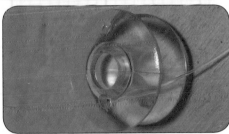

Step 4: Tape Two Cards Together

The structure for the grappling hook is basically just the credit card itself. So in order to keep it stiff and strong, I used double-sided tape to stick two cards together.

Step 5: Drill Holes

Drill holes in the card for the hook launcher (rubber band) and the binding post that will hold the cable spool (sewing bobbin).

Step 6: Attatch Spool to Card

Attach the bobbin to the card using the binding post, and then loop the rubber band through the top hole to create the elastic launcher. I made a slight dimple in the back edge of the card that the rubber band fits into, which allows me to easily stow the grappling hook when it's not in use.

The last steps are to go shoot at stuff, try to reel it in, and to have fun!

Tiny Shooter

By mikroGanesh
(http://www.instructables.com/
id/lollipop-stick-gun/)

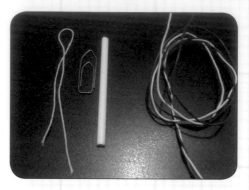

Shoots small bits of pencil tips/toothpicks and stuff as ammo! One can make this in less than 15 minutes with stuff around. Take safety precautions while making and using the shooter as it shoots the ammo really far.

Step 1: In Action
Step 2: Materials

- Lollipop stick/tubing/empty ballpoint refill
- Paperclip
- Thin elastic rubber band
- Wire
- Pin
- Needle-nose pliers to shape and cut the wire

Step 3: Getting Started

Take the paperclip, open it, and make the plunger as shown. Shape a piece of wire to make the gun end.

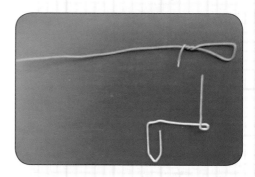

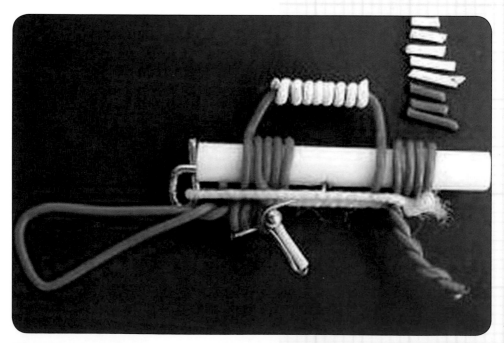

Step 4: Mechanism—Part 1

Cut the plunger using the pliers. Tie the elastic band to get a smaller rubber band. Cut the lollipop tube in half, making sure it is bigger than our plunger. Make a tiny hole in the area shown on the tube. For holding the trigger, make a small loop in the gun-end wire by rolling it around a paper pin.

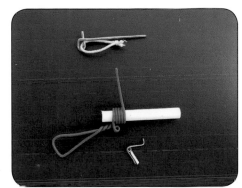

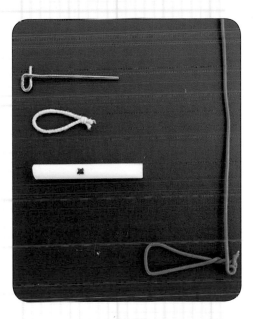

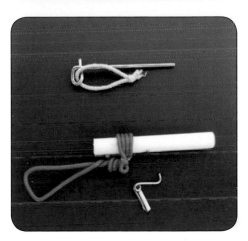

Step 5: Mechanism—Part 2

Pass the rubber band through the plunger end. Make a trigger by rolling the wire with a loop in the center. Tie up the gun-end wire as shown.

Step 6: Trigger Mechanism

Making the trigger mechanism is a bit tricky. Use a pin to hold the trigger in position, as shown below. This trigger should be able to hold the plunger when the rubber band mechanism is pulled.

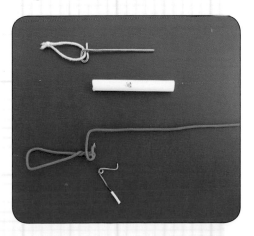

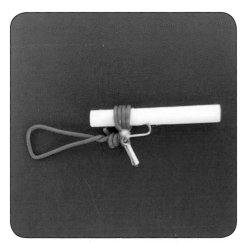

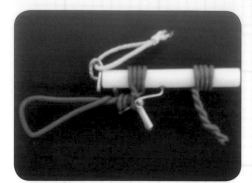

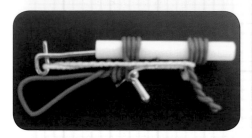

Step 8: Finishing Touches

The trigger needs to be pressed in the aperture so as to hold the plunger when armed. When pulled, it can shoot your ammo. You can also use a tiny rubber band to press the trigger in place (not shown here). Use your imagination and design other accessories like gun sights, handles, etc.

Step 7: Assembly

Take a bit of wire and securely tie it to make a kind of magazine. This will serve to hold the rubber mechanism in place. Assemble as indicated and pull to arm the shooter.

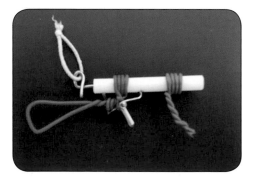

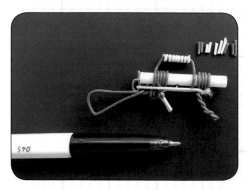

The MacGyver Gun(s)

By jacob13
(http://www.instructables.com/
id/The-MacGyver-Guns/)

In this instructable, I will show you how to make three different, extremely easy-to-make "projectile shooters" from highlighters, pens, and a little bit of fire. I made about ten more while I was waiting for the pictures to upload to make this.

WARNING: DO NOT SHOOT ANY OF THESE GUNS AT ANY LIVING THING. I AM NOT RESPONSIBLE FOR ANY BURNS, INJURIES, OR ANY KIND OF BAD LUCK RESULTING FROM THE USE OF THE PRODUCTS OF THIS INSTRUCTABLE FOR ANY REASON.

Now, for the fun part!

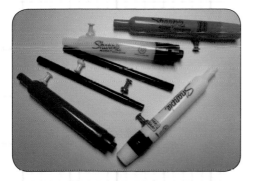

Step 1: Materials

To make all three of these, you will need the following, plus a little creativity to make a stand, but that comes later.

- Superglue
- Pt least two Sharpie highlighters
- Paper Mate "M" pens (no substitutions)
- Scissors
- Thumbtacks (not shown)
- Screw that fits in the small end of the highlighter
- Electrical tape
- Matches (not shown)
- A way to attach the screw to something solid (shown at the end)
- Various aerosol sprays (Experiment and see which one works best for you.)
- Needle-nose pliers

Step 2: Gun #1

The pictures in each step do the real explaining; pictures are worth thousands of words.

This gunis the one that shoots the little cap.

First, you need to disassemble the highlighter; then you can throw away any inky pieces (the tip and the cartridge). Then, take the cap of the highlighter and use the scissors to make a hole the same size as the little part on the end of the cap (see image). Now, take the cap and shove it as far as it will go into the big end of the highlighter, taking care not to crack it. Superglue it in place. While that dries, take the little end cap (the "projectile"), cover it in a few layers of the electrical tape, and fold over the ends. This makes it airtight so there is no

55

"blow by" when it fires. After that, put some electrical tape over the superglue bond and put the "projectile" on the end. Carefully insert the thumbtack close to but not on the small end of the highlighter.

See the "Firing the MacGyver Guns" step if you want to make just this; if you want to make the rest, read on!

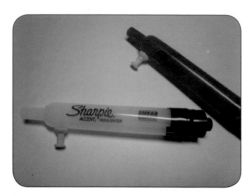

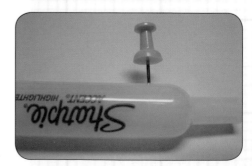

Step 3: Gun #2

This (highlighter) one shoots whatever you put in it.

First disassemble the highlighter and throw away the inky parts (just like before). Now, put the little end cap back exactly where you just took it from, put a small hole in the center, and superglue it in place. *Before* you superglue, put a small hole in the cap just like in gun #1. *Quickly*, before the superglue dries, put the cap on as if you were using the highlighter normally and put more glue around it. Then, carefully put a thumbtack close to but not on the cap and cover the superglue with electrical tape.

Skip to the Firing step, or read on to make the most MacGyverish gun yet!

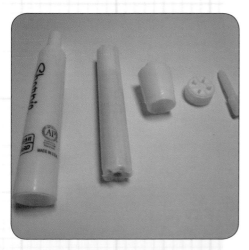

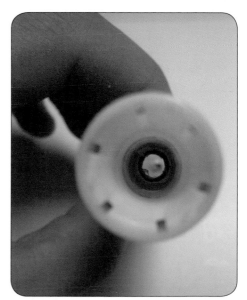

Step 4: Gun #3

This is the best one in my opinion. This one shoots whatever you put in it, and you can make a million in about ten minutes. It takes only scissors and a thumbtack to make.

First, take out the whole ink assembly, leaving the empty pen. Now, using scissors, pop out the little thingy in the end (make a hole). Then, carefully insert a thumbtack into the end you made the hole in.

Finally, time for the really fun part!

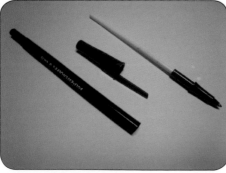

Step 5: Firing the MacGyver Guns

Now, first I need to say that for safety reasons, we only used each one once. The price of pens is way less than the price of having one explode in your hand, which is also why we didn't hold ours but improvised a tripod. If you don't happen to have a broken drum stand, just put some screws through a piece of wood and stick it in the ground. Whatever works. Also, please be careful when lighting it, and use earplugs, safety glasses, and other safety equipment as you so desire.

Okay. The procedure is simple. Screw it on, spray a *short* burst of axe, air freshener, etc, into the barrel, then shove whatever you are firing onto the end. You have to work fast so the propellant won't evaporate into the air. Now take out the thumbtack and hold up a lit match or lighter to the small hole, and KEEP YOUR HAND BACK! Don't be stupid and hold your hand right in front of the fire hole; keep it up a little bit. Same goes for the path of the projectile.

You may have to try a couple of times for it to actually work. Good Luck!

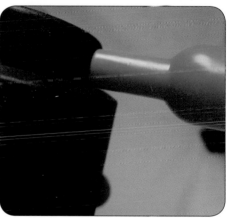

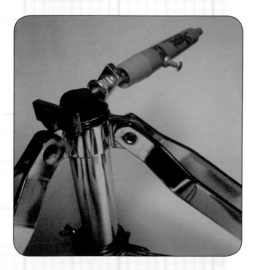

Quick and Easy Office Darts

By fjordcarver
(http://www.instructables.com/
id/Quick-and-Easy-Office-Darts/)

DISCLAIMER: THESE DARTS CAN BE DANGEROUS. THEY ARE DARTS.

Okay they are darts, they are great for throwing. Please don't throw them at anyone. You will probably hurt them.

They are really easy to make and discrete to use. By discrete, I do not mean that you can sneak up on a friend or enemy, I mean that they will stick into loads of stuff while leaving behind very little evidence. The wall won't be covered in discernible holes.

They are about as accurate as a regular dart-board dart, which is to say as accurate as you are.

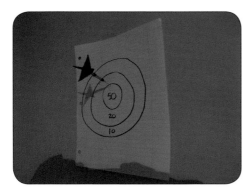

Step 1: Stuff You Need

You will need to collect a few things.
- 4 toothpicks (check the cafeteria)
- 1 business card
- A sheet of paper (for the dartboard)
- Needle and thread (ask around; one of your coworkers might have a small sewing kit on their person)
- A small piece of tape (not required . . . helpful)

Alternatively, you could substitute out just about all of the parts. A sharpened length of paperclip instead of a pin, matchsticks, tape—but I will show you my technique. It works well, and the darts have a ninja appeal.

Step 2: Shafted

To make the shaft of the dart, you need to connect the four toothpicks together lengthwise very tightly.

Begin by positioning the toothpicks together and placing a small piece of tape just to hold them while you get the thread started.

Tie the thread around the cluster around ⅓ of the way up the toothpick, and then wrap it as tightly as you can for a bunch of turns (30 or more). Once you are satisfied that it is secure, tie off a knot *without* allowing the thread to loosen.

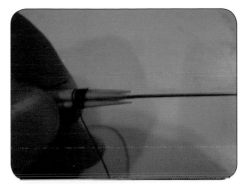

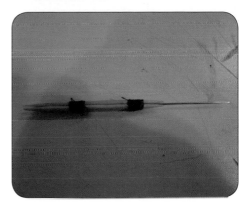

Step 3: Eye of the Needle

Now, on to the other end. Remove your tape, and start wrapping another thread close to the end. If you are using rounded toothpicks, as I am, then go to the point where the toothpick begins to taper. Just a few turns at this point. We want it snug, but not too tight yet.

Leaving it a little loose, stop winding and set your sewing needle into position. You want it to be held in the center of the four toothpicks. It should be inserted in only a little ways, just past your initial winding.

Once you are satisfied, continue winding, now as tightly as you can without snapping the thread. As before, do 30 turns or more, and then tie it off.

There, you already should have a decent looking harpoon. I bet this would shoot nicely out of a marker tube with some elastics, too.

Let's go on to make the fins.

Step 4: Fishy . . . erm . . . Finny

Cut your business card to a square (roughly will do fine). Fold it in half to create a triangle. Fold that triangle in half. Fold that triangle in half, again. Unfold it all and work each second segment into the center, creating a beautiful set of fins for your new dart. Slide it into position on your dart, just like a real one. Go on then, give it a toss.

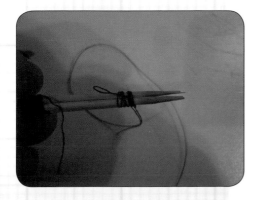

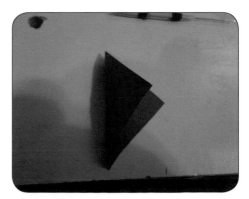

Step 5: Play!

Your dart is finished, now go play with it. These little beauties will stick into a lot of stuff. They are sharp and well balanced. Getting a game set up is as simple as drawing up a board, taping it to almost any wall, and throwing darts. Make a set of three and get an office tournament going.

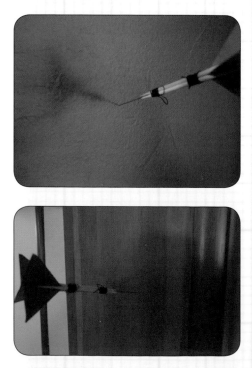

Office Stationery Darts

By logghi
(http://www.instructables.com/
id/Office-Stationary-Darts/)

This Instructable will tell you how to make some simple little darts out of household or office stationery.

Step 1: Materials
- Press tacks
- Paperclips
- Elastic bands
- 3in × 3in sticky notes
- Cardboard

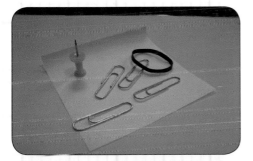

Step 2: Attaching the Clips

Hold the clips around the tack with one hand, and wrap around the elastic band with the other to keep it in place. This is the hardest part. If you struggle at first, try attaching one at a time (although you will need more bands to do this).

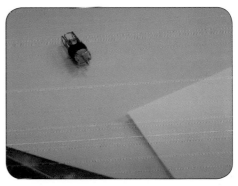

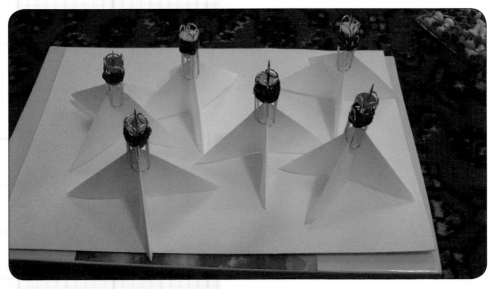

63

Step 4: Adding the Flights

Simply slide the flights in between the paperclips at the loose end.

Step 3: Making the Flights

Fold the sticky note in half to make a rectangle, then unfold again. Then fold in half to make a triangle, then unfold again. Then fold into a triangle once more the other way. These are the base folds. Fold in half along the first base fold (into a rectangle). Next, take one of the top corners (one that's folded) and pull down into the middle, then repeat on the other side. Even out the sides. It's very simple to do, but it is hard to demonstrate in the form of text. Luckily, I can provide a picture.

Step 5: Boards

So, now you've got your darts all lined up, what to throw them at? A board would be a good idea, and cardboard works perfectly. You can make up your own designs. I just used a cardboard box to demonstrate.

Rubber Band Shooter

By saul
(http://www.instructables.com/
id/Rubber-Band-Shooter/)

You need nothing but your hand and a rubber band to go gun slinging around the house or office.

Step 1:

Choose your rubber band and prepare your hand.

Step 2:

Load one end of the rubber band between pinky and palm.

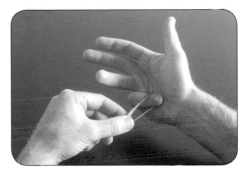

Step 3:

Loop other end of the rubber band around behind your thumb while making a pistol with your hand.

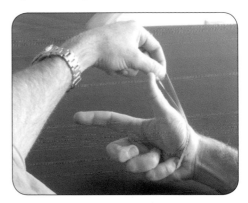

Step 4:

Hook loose end of the rubber band on your forefinger—now you are loaded.

Centrifugal Airsoft Pen Machine Gun

By pastprimitive
(http://www.instructables.com/
id/Centrifugal-Airsoft-Pen-
Machine-Gun/)

Made almost exclusively from office supplies, this centrifugal machine gun is the perfect device for booby trapping beloved objects that coworkers have a tendency to take.

So it's more of an airsoft grenade in this form, except, with a little more time and without much trouble, you could get it to shoot in the same general spot each time. I still think it's great fun to play with, though, even with its shoot everything in sight mode. In the future, I would like to add a much larger hopper, but for now this suits my purposes.

Disclaimer: Don't hurt yourself, or others.

Step 1: Materials and Tools

Materials
- 4 large paperclips
- 2 disposable ballpoint pens
- 1 nine-volt battery
- 1 small dc motor (the faster the better)
- 1 piece of paper
- 1 magnet
- Corrugated cardboard
- Aluminum foil
- Tape
- Double-sided tape
- Airsoft ammo or other small round object that will freely fit inside of the disposable pens

Tools
- X-acto knife
- Needle-nose pliers
- Scissors
- Awesomeness

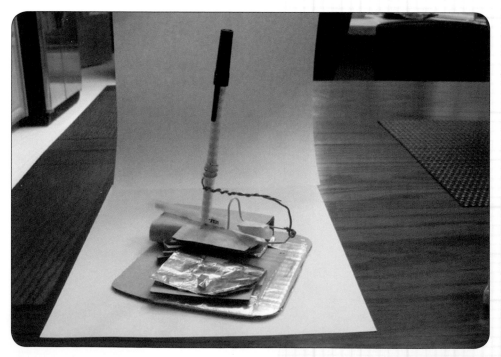

Step 2: Build Your Barrel

Take apart one ballpoint pen and harvest the body. It should be big enough to allow airsoft rounds to roll through freely. Both ends should be open. On some brands, you may need to cut off the butt of the pen to open both ends up.

Using an X-acto knife or if, like me, you have access to a mill and enjoy overkill, cut out a section that is about 0.6 inch long and will allow airsoft rounds to drop in and roll out either end of the ballpoint pen body without jamming.

Drill a hole in the center of the pen body opposite of the hole you just cut (see pictures for reference). The hole should be slightly smaller than the diameter of your DC motor drive shaft (because that is where the barrel will be mounted).

Note: You will notice in one of the pictures that I have cut out a small section from another pen body to reinforce the section of the barrel we cut out. In retrospect I feel this is unnecessary.

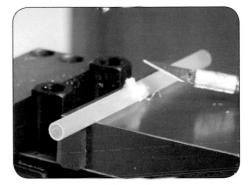

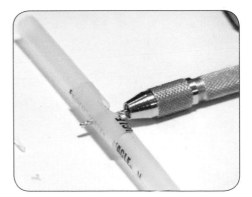

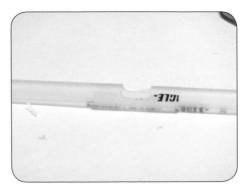

Step 3: Make the Magnetic Trip Switch

I thought the best switch to use for this would be an aluminum foil magnetic switch that I dreamed up on the fly. This will essentially allow you to put a spacer in between the switch that, when pulled out (e.g. with fishing line), will allow the magnet to stick to the paperclip and close the circuit. Ignore the binder clips; they turned out to be unnecessary.

Take a small piece of paper and tape a paperclip on one end.

Tape a piece of aluminum foil over the paperclip. Leave enough aluminum foil to wrap around on both sides of the paper. Be sure to leave as much of the aluminum foil exposed as possible. You will need one side on the bottom that has no tape on it so you can connect it into the circuit later on.

Tape a second piece of aluminum foil on the other end of the piece of paper, being sure to leave plenty of space in-between the two pieces of aluminum foil. Make sure that, when folded in half, the aluminum foil on the non-paperclip side is not covered with tape so they can make contact with each other to complete the circuit.

Tape a magnet onto the non-paperclip side, so that when the switch is folded in half the magnet will sandwich the two aluminum-foil-covered sides together.

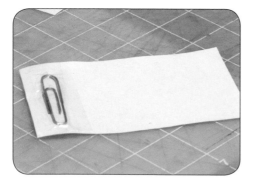

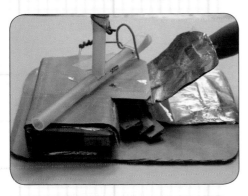

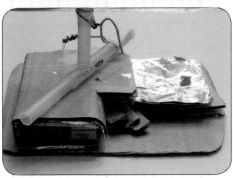

Step 4: Build Your Paperclip Pen Hopper and Add a Timing Bump Switch

The hopper is made from another disposable ballpoint pen with the ballpoint and ink well assembly taken out. I used the cap to prevent ammo from bouncing out.

The following steps will describe how to build and attached the bump switch timer to the barrel:

1. Take a large paperclip and bend the small U away from the large U into what looks like a number 8.
2. Bend the paperclip into an L shape as pictured.
3. Tape the small U to the top of our barrel with your favorite tape of choice. Masking tape works well for this.

To build the hopper holder:

1. Take one large paperclip and straighten.

2. Then, using needle-nose pliers, bend into a U shape. Leave plenty of length on the uprights of your U. They will stick in to the corrugated cardboard and allow us to position the hopper right where it needs to be. The extra length also allows it to be positioned far enough away so that the barrel will not swing into our hopper holder.
3. Take another large paperclip and straighten.
4. Using the needle-nose pliers, wrap one end around the corner of the U we just made. Wrap enough times so that the two paperclips will not shift relative to each other.
5. Bend the paperclip we just wrapped around our U into an L shape.
6. Take another large paperclip and straighten.
7. Wrap around the L we just made to extend the length of the L and give you enough to wrap around the hopper to secure it tightly.

Step 5: Build the Motor Platform and Circuits

The motor platform is built from two pieces of corrugated cardboard. I secured the motor to the cardboard by saving the mounting screws from the motor that I harvested from a broken portable DVD player. After putting a piece of tape on the top of the cardboard to prevent tear-through, I poked three small holes that corresponded with the drive shaft and two motor mounting holes and screwed the motor on with the aforementioned screws.

To create the circuit that would connect the battery and motor to the magnetic trip switch, I used a marker and drew out the circuit on the cardboard first. Then, I laid double-sided tape over the lines I drew. After that, I placed a piece of aluminum foil over the double-sided tape so no double-sided tape was left uncovered. Using an X-acto knife, I cut out the aluminum foil that was not connected to the double-sided tape. Then, I covered the circuit with clear tape to prevent accidental shorts. I *did not* cover the ends of the circuit where I needed to make connections.

Note: I really like the aluminum foil/ double-sided tape combination for a circuit. While I am sure it's been done, it was new to me, and I was proud that I thought of it on my own.

I mounted the motor/9 volt battery assembly and the magnetic trip switch with the double-sided tape. I used clear tape to secure all the motor leads and other connections down. I also used tape to secure the cardboard around the 9 volt battery.

Note: While you are working with the magnetic trip switch, you should place a piece of cardboard in-between so that the switch can't close the circuit.

Step 6: Assembly and Deployment

To assemble the machine:

1. Press fit barrel onto drive shaft of motor.
2. Insert paperclip hopper holder into the side of corrugated cardboard.
3. Adjust paperclip hopper holder until the hopper rests in the center of your barrel opening.
4. Adjust hopper to hang low enough that, when it's filled with airsoft rounds, they do not roll out of the barrel. But when the bump switch rotates under the hopper holder, it slightly bumps the hopper up, allowing a round to roll out of the barrel.

Find something to hide your centrifugal booby trap machine gun in. I know the box I used is lame. I simply ran out of time before I needed to post this for the weekly challenge. You can use anything that will cover the device. Have a small piece of cardboard and fishing line attached to it so that you can place the cardboard in between the magnetic trip switch.

Set the trap and enjoy. When the item is removed by unsuspecting victims, the cardboard will be removed and the magnetic trip switch will close. Mwha ha ha! Let the airsoft madness begin. Okay . . . mine wasn't really powerful enough to make the airsoft round hurt or cause that much madness. But the airsoft pellets are really annoying to pick up. And actually I am glad they didn't hurt; booby traps that hurt are not fun.

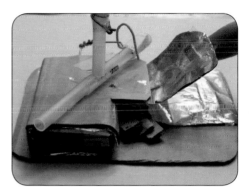

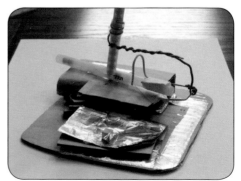

shooters and darts

71

How to Make the EPG (Echo Pen Gun)

By my_2_cents
(http://www.instructables.com/
id/how-to-make-a-pen-gun/)

The EPG ("Echo1 Pen Gun") shoots BB's and almost anything that can fit inside the pen gun smoothly. Unlike other pen guns, this gun can be used as an ordinary pen, using it to right your English essay. Spring-powered, this classroom riot device can shoot 15' with ease, an amazing feat considering it is shooting a BB.

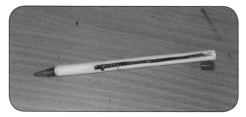

Step 1: Equipment and Materials

- Hot glue gun
- Pliers
- Paperclip
- Knife
- Hack saw or scissors
- BIC pen
- Filer
- Sandpaper
- Springs

Step 2

Disassemble the pen so that you only have the tube. Remove the yellow tip from the blue connector thing (the yellow tip is connected to the Ink tube). Remove the blue connector. Remove the end cap (I used a screwed driver).

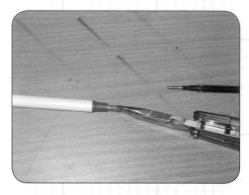

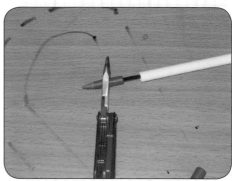

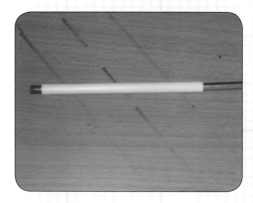

Step 3

Cut the blue connector at the point where the scissors are placed in the image. Sand and file the surfaces that have been cut. Cut the bottom part of the blue connector just below the BIC logo. Afterwards, file and sand it. You will only need the part without the BIC logo. Hot glue the blue connector bit that fits inside the pen tube. (Push it in so the whole thing is inside the tube, just at one end. The picture next will display what I mean.)

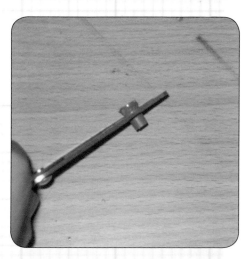

73

Step 4

Dig a hole into the tube as shown. Start sinking the knife into the pen tube and sliding it forwards to create a long slot. Now, start carving the edges and filing it so it becomes wider. It should be 3 mm wide, and the length will vary depending on how many springs the pen gun contains. Sand edges so it is smooth and remove unnecessary pieces of plastic hanging on the edges.

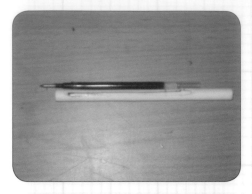

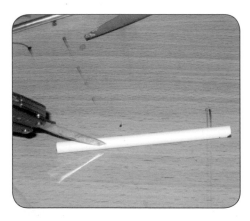

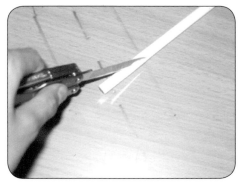

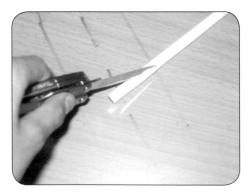

Step 5

Connect the blue connector that was cut earlier to the yellow tip. Pull the yellow tip from the ink tube. Hot glue it back together so it has a tighter and stickier fit. Remove any dispensable glue. Put the ink tube inside the pen tube. On the ink tube, just before it reaches the top of the slot that was cut out, create a small hole from a thumb tack or something, where one end of a paperclip can fit in it. Get a paperclip and cut it so it's about 3 cm to 4 cm. Then, bend it so it is about a right angle side of the right angle smaller than the other.

Step 6: Step 5

While your ink tube is inside the pen tube, insert your springs. If your springs do not reach higher than the hole you made on the ink tube for the paperclip, simply insert the smaller side of the right angled paperclip into the ink tube. If your spring height is beyond the hole that was made on the ink tube, simply take a skewer and push the spring down so it's under the hole (compressing the springs) and then insert your paperclip. Pull the yellow tip so that the springs fully compress. Mark the point on the pen where the ink tube cannot possibly go down any further. Mark that point with a permanent marker. Cut the hole like in the picture below.

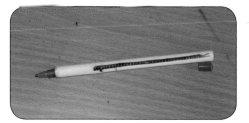

Step 7

If you do not possess BB's, you can create something similar by making solder balls or balls out of glue (produced by the hot glue gun).

Step 8

Pull the paper clip down and twist it to the side hole at the point where the springs are fully compressed. Once you have done that, flick the paperclip out of the hole; it should fly up, shooting anything inside the pen gun.

Mechanical Pencil Gun

By beam
(http://www.instructables.com/
id/Mechanical-Pencil-Gun/)

An easy-to-make office weapon capable of firing anything that will fit in the barrel.

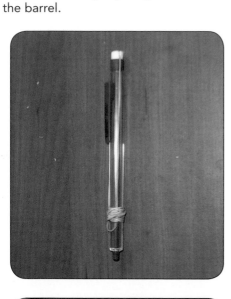

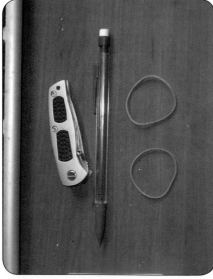

Step 1: Gather Materials

All you need is a BIC mechanical pencil and two rubber bands. Pencils by BIC are perfectly suited to this (I haven't tried any other models yet). You also need a knife/razor to make an incision later.

Step 2: The Barrel

To make the barrel, you first need to get rid of the writing cone. The writing cone is the gray cone attached to the clear cylinder in the picture in step one. I find that the easiest way to do this is to let the cone hang off the edge of a desk, and break it off with your palm. Once the cone is off, you should be able to pull the eraser shaft out.

Step 3: Rubber Bands

To attach the rubber band, first put one end around the pocket clip on the barrel. Then, stretch the other end out to the opposite end of the barrel. Once you do that, you can use the second rubber band to tie it to the barrel.

Step 4: Firing Mechanism

Get the eraser shaft and make an incision with your blade through the center of the eraser, coming from the top. You want to split it, not cut it off. Then, take the rubber band end off of the clip, and slide it into the notch you've made in the eraser.

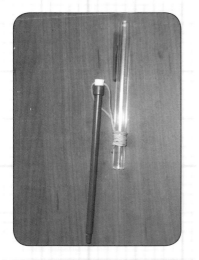

Step 5: Completion

With the rubber band attached to the eraser shaft, slide it back into the barrel. The gun is now complete. To fire, pull back the eraser shaft, load ammunition into the muzzle, and release.

Step 6: Final Notes and Modification Suggestions

The gun is pretty powerful, but its potential is defined by the type of bands you use. High-tension bands make the gun much more powerful. However, it does have its shortcomings. Multiple impacts from the eraser shaft to the barrel chip away at the barrel, eventually making it useless. It has also got a lot of kick, and it's pretty uncomfortable to fire if you're using really strong bands (even though some of the bands I used could put a BB through a soda can). The way I described is the bare-bones assembly. There are many modifications that could increase the longevity of the gun and make it more powerful. On my gun, I took the clip off of the barrel, wrapped the entire barrel in electrician's tape, and proceeded from there. That reduces chipping from the firing mechanism. I also wrapped the eraser notch assembly with tape (just in case, and it makes the gun look more uniform). There is also a part of the eraser shaft that is not as wide as the rest; I cut it off and filed it down, so that the hammer takes up the whole width of the barrel and leaves some space in the muzzle for ammunition, even when the hammer isn't pulled back. Finally, at the firing end in the clear shaft, the opening isn't as wide. You can shave the excess plastic off to make for a uniform barrel width.

Turn a Mousetrap into a Powerful Handgun

By The King of Random
(http://www.instructables.com/
id/Turn-a-Mousetrap-into-a-
Powerful-Handgun/)

Here's how to turn a mousetrap into a fun little handgun that shoots up to 40'! This is a great project because it can be made with simple materials, very basic tools, and a minimal amount of time!

MOUSETRAP HAND-GUN

Step 1: What You Will Need

This pack of two mousetraps was only $0.98 from "Lowes" Home Improvement store! Aside from those, all you're going to need are:

- 2 small screws (like the kind on your door hinges)
- A small piece of 2" × 2"

Suggested tools to make the job easier are:

- Screwdriver
- Needle-nose pliers
- Wire snips

Step 2: Prepare the Mousetrap

Cut the piece of wood so that it fits comfortably in your hand, then drill three holes with a 1/8" drill bit in the places shown in the picture. The two screws will secure the trap to the wood handle. Make sure you leave just a little overhang at the back.

Step 3: Make the Firing Mechanism

The firing mechanism is made by modifying the locking pin into a squeeze-pull trigger. Modify the locking pin so that it's trimmed down in a way that it overlaps the most forward hole you drilled, then bend the tip of the pin up at a 45° angle.

The next step is to use the locking pin from the other trap as the trigger. Push the pin up through the bottom of the hole, then trim it flush with the top of the spring, and then bend it over in a an n shape. This will prevent it from slipping back down through the hole.

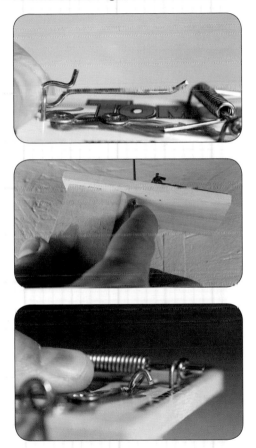

Step 4: Add the Launching Pad

The bait pad can be converted into a launching platform that will shoot any type of small ammunition! With the trap hammer relaxed, clip the bait pad with the hooks facing upward, then carefully lift the hammer, tuck the pad underneath, and relax the hammer back down onto the trap base. Your gun is finished, and ready for testing!

Step 5: Loading the Mousetrap Gun

To cock the gun, pull the hammer back in the same way you would set the mousetrap. Carefully overlap the locking pin, and set the tip so that it holds firm in the hook you made on the trigger pin. Be careful with this step and make sure your fingers are clear, because if the pin slips, the trap hammer will snap over and give your fingers a smack. I made a little target for practice. In the next step you'll see different types of ammo that work well for shooting.

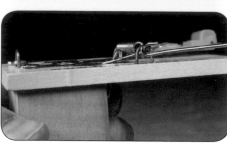

Step 6: Types of Ammunition

I found that Airsoft BB's work perfectly! The little divot in the center of the pad is perfectly situated to shoot these BB's straight forward and at distances up to 40'! They are small and fast and don't do too much damage to anything they hit. Other types of ammunition I found work well are

- pennies
- small rocks
- plastic bottle caps
- and glass beads.

Basically any item that's small and dense works great!

Moving the ammo forward on the pad makes the gun shoot low and fast, like a gun. Shifting the ammo rearward causes the object to be launched high and far, like a catapult. You can play around with different positions to see how your shooting patterns are affected.

Step 7: Finished

This simple device launches projectiles with both power and precision. The cost was about $1.00. Just for fun, I made a third gun and painted it black to see how it would contrast with the yellow launch pad.

The Best Damn Pen Shooter Period

By kargod
(http://www.instructables.com/
id/The-Best-Damn-Pen-Shooter-
Period./)

This is *a warning*. Do *not* under *any circumstances* point this at anybody or any living creature. It's a very strong little pen shooter and can leave more than a mark. I am not going to be held accountable for your actions, so if you are not mature enough to handle this carefully . . . turn away *now*.

Now for the good stuff.This is a fun and easy (and cheap) little toy that I invented the other day. It's very strong and shoots very far.

Tools and Materials
- 1 Office Depot ballpoint pen—very cheap—1 dozen for $0.89 (this might work with other pens, but I haven't tried)
- 1 rubber band of medium length
- Some string
- Scissors

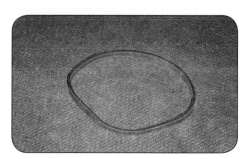

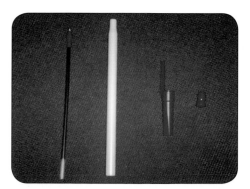

Step 1: Making the Barrel

Pull the writing end and the little plug on the back of the pen off. This is a very easy step; if you can't figure it out, you *lose*. Please try again.

Step 2: Placing the Rubber Band

The ideal way to place the rubber band is to have it crossed across the pen (as shown). You want to make sure that the rubber band lies only about 1.5" past the firing end when it is fully stretched. Note: The firing end is the end opposite the side you write with. It's the one with the wider hole.

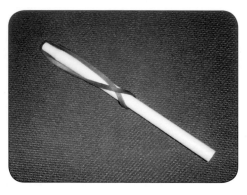

Step 3: Securing the Rubber Band

Use the string to tightly wrap around the rubber band. How much string you use and where you place it will affect how your rubber band stretches. Tie the string off at the end so it won't come loose.

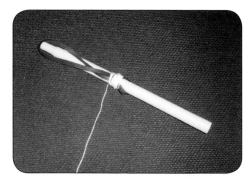

Step 4: Loading the Ammo

Use the ink cartridge as the ammo. Insert it into the wide hole of the barrel so that the pointy end goes in last. Let it slide all the way to the bottom. If you

are using an Office Depot pen, the ink cartridge will fit in there very nicely.

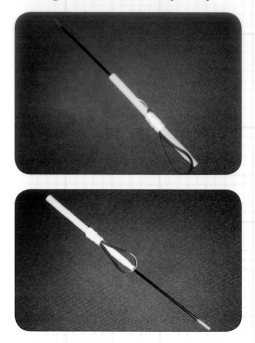

Step 5: Firing

Grab the rubber band and the bottom of the ink cartridge, pull straight back, and release. Note: If you pull too tightly, the ink cartridge might:
a) break within the pen, thus making a big mess
   or
b) fly too hard and explode as it hits a rigid object, thus making a big mess.

If you made this properly, it should fire around 30' at least. Make modifications to your rubber band as needed. Have fun and be safe.

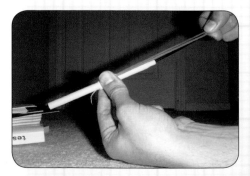

Blowgun
By casvandegoor
(http://www.instructables.com/
id/blow-gun-1/)

This is the most simple toy to have hours of fun with!

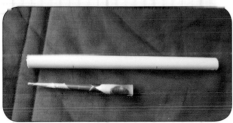

Step 1: Materials
- PVC tube: diameter of 1 cm; length can range from 20 to 100 cm. Longer barrels are more accurate but harder to carry around in combat and require a longer breathe to operate.
- Magazine page
- Adhesive tape
- A pair of scissors
- Sandpaper

Step 2: Barrel
Saw a piece to length that suits you and make the cut edge nice and smooth with sandpaper.

Step 3: Projectile
Cut the magazine page into a long strip with a width of 5 to 8 cm. Turn the strip of paper into a cone. Put adhesive tape on the apex to keep the paper together. Slide the cone into the barrel and trim its end.

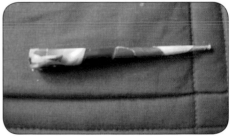

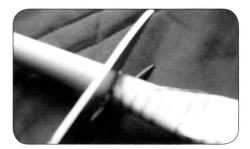

Step 4: Blow
Let's roll! Put the cone into the tube, aim, and blow. Wear safety goggles when playing with your friends. Have fun!

This Instructable will teach you how to create an automatic marshmallow gun out of ½" PVC pipe.

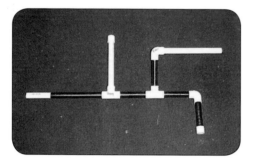

Step 1: Materials
- 2.5" PVC caps
- 2.5" PVC elbows
- 2.5" PVC tees
- 4 5" sections of ½" PVC pipe
- 1 11" PVC pipe (barrel)
- 1 8" PVC pipe (hopper)
- 1 9" PVC pipe (mouth piece)
- cotton balls
- Optional: electrical tape (for looks)

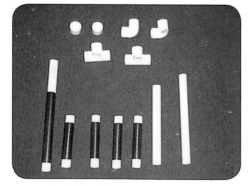

Step 2: Assembling Mouthpiece
To make the mouthpiece, you will need to connect the 9" pipe to an elbow. Connect that to a 5" section and connect that to a tee.

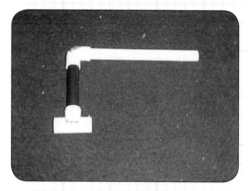

Step 3: Assembling Hopper
To make the hopper, you will need to attach a cap to the 8" pipe. Then, on the other end, attach a tee and, to that, attach a 5" section.

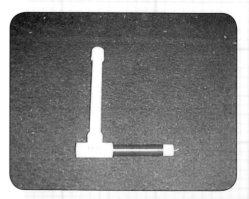

Step 4: Assembling Handle

To make the handle, you will need to attach two 5" pieces to an elbow and put a cap on one of them. The piece without the cap needs to be stuffed with cotton balls. The other piece needs to remain hollow so you can fill it with marshmallows (cannot hold very many but why not?).

Step 5: Put It All Together

In this step, we will put all the pieces together and attach the barrel.

Step 6: If There Was Any Confusion

Just in case you didn't understand anything, here is a more detailed picture if everything.

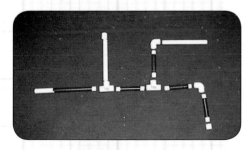

Step 7: Usage

In order to use this gun, you first need to load the hopper (8" pipe) with mini marshmallows (mine held fifteen). Then you need to reattach to gun, aim in a safe direction, and blow continuously through the mouthpiece. If all went well, all fifteen marshmallows should have left the barrel. Mine shoots a good 20 yards.

Step 8: Modification

There are many improvements that can be done to this gun. I wrapped electric tape around mine to give it a better appearance. You could also put another tee behind the hopper, facing down, and attach another handle. You could adjust the length of the pipes for a bigger or smaller gun. There are an infinite amount of possibilities.

Step 9: Ammunition

This gun is designed to shoot miniature marshmallows.

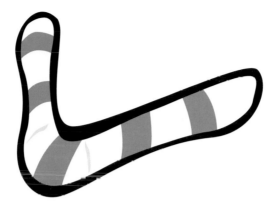

Section 4

Miscellaneous

- -

Not all office supplies are destined to be destructive—sometimes all you want is some fun to entertain yourself at work. This final chapter covers projects that should mostly be used as a remedy to stop you from falling asleep during those long conference calls. Make a boomerang or a mini Skee ball game, or . . . who are we kidding? This chapter also has a few more weapons thrown in for the heck of it as well! Make a shrapnel-tossing booby trap and nunchucku made from magazines. Let's face it, using office supplies for anything but weapons means you'll be the first crushed in the inevitable water-cooler melee.

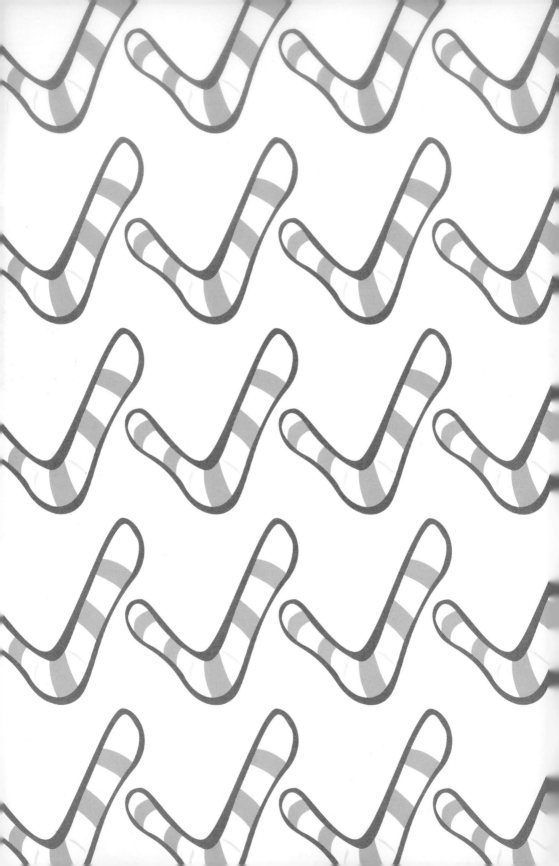

Rubber Band- Powered Bug

By computergeek
(http://www.instructables.com/
id/Rubber-Band-Powered-Bug/)

This Iinstructable is on how to build a rubber-band-powered bug, which is very similar to a "bristle bot." The only difference is that it's not on a toothbrush and not battery powered. (More green power!) Also, if you carry around weird stuff (I do!) like a paperclip, a rubber band, wire, and pliers, you can build one anywhere!

Step 1: Stuff You Need:
- Large paperclip
- Small paperclip
- Small rubber band about 1 inch long
- 5 in wire or twist tie
- Small counterweight (I used a capacitor). You don't really need this, but it works better with it.
- Pliers
- Hot glue

Step 2: Make the Body (Rubber Band Holder)

To make the legs: Unbend the large paperclip some. Make a small notch in the end of the paperclip. Following the pictures, make a series of 90 degree bends in the large paperclip. First, bend the paperclip ¼ inch from the end with the notch in it. Make another bend ¾ inch from the last bend. Then make three more, each ¼ inch from the previous bend. Finally, make another bend 1 inch from the last bend. You may want to straighten out the paperclip the rest of the way. Mark 1 inch from the last bend and cut off the excess. Strip off the plastic coating from the last bend to the end. Start a loop ½ inch from the last bend. and finish it. I used the rest of the paperclip to make it nice and round. The body is done and the loop is complete.

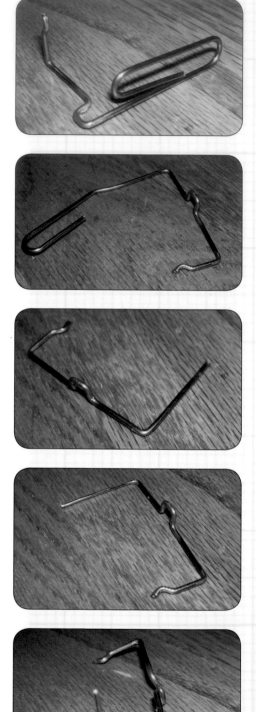

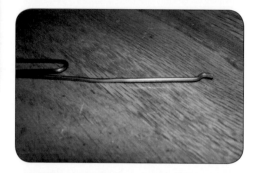

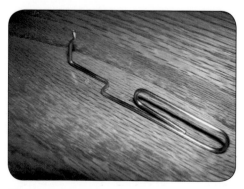

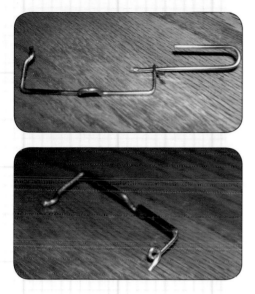

Step 3: Make the Counterweight Arm

Unbend the small paperclip and put a small hook in one end. Make a 90 degree bend ⅜ inch from the end of the hook. Make a mark at 1 inch from the last bend and trim off the excess. Start coiling the end of the paperclip. Finish up the coil and feed the hook through the loop on the body. Attach the rubber band from the hook to the notch on the body. Put some hot glue on your counterweight and glue it on.

miscellaneous

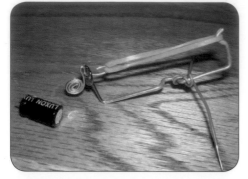

Step 4: Attach the Legs

Make one loop by the bend closest to the rubber band notch. Make one more loop, then two more loops. You are now ready for the hot glue. Note: You don't need to hot glue the legs; they stay on fine like this without it. But it's nice to do.

Step 5: Have Fun!

To use a rubber-band-powered bug, just wind it up and let it go! Experiment which way of winding works best for you. I found that winding it up counter-clockwise so it turns clockwise works pretty good. So, like the title says, have fun!

Office Booby Trap

By PocketSized
(http://www.instructables
.com/id/Office-Booby-
trap/)

This is a fun little booby trap that fires objects when a trip wire is pulled. It is made from a few simple items that can be found around the office or home. Needless to say, be careful what you fire at people.

Step 1: What You Will Need

- 3 paperclips
- Bottle top
- Rubber band
- Pliers (needle-nose)
- Ruler
- String
- 2 drawing pins

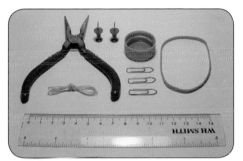

Step 2: Straighten the Paperclips

Using your pliers, straighten the 3 paper clips.

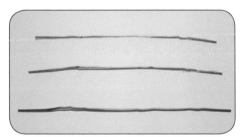

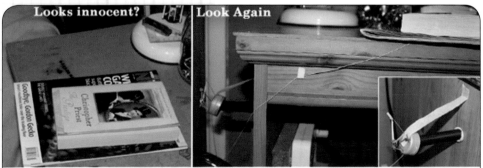

Looks innocent? **Look Again**

Why limit yourself to making it shoot straight at the person?

Here the Booby Trap has been loaded with lots of U shaped staples and is rigged to fire like a mortar at whoever lifts the book.
Spraying the book theif with metal staples.

Step 3: Make Four Holes in the Bottle Top

Turn the bottle top upwards and then, using one of the drawing pins, make 2 holes at either end. Make the holes at one end approximately 2 cm apart, and at the other end 1.5 cm apart.

Step 4: Bend a Paperclip and Insert into Bottle Cap

Now bend one of the paper clips using the pliers so that there is a 2 cm gap in the middle of the two "arms." This is going to be pushed through the holes in the bottle cap that are 2 cm apart, so that the arms point out the top.

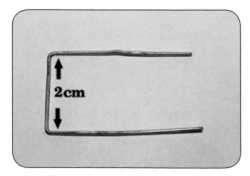

Step 5: Bend the Arms and Attach the Rubber Band

Bend both the arms outwards slightly so they are at a 45-degree angle. To attach the rubber band to the arms, we need to roughly cut out a 4 cm section of the rubber band and tie a knot in each end. Now rest the rubber band between the tips of the two arms, bend the tips of the arms around the rubber band, and clamp them down. Make sure there is no room for the knots to slip though. An image of the finished result of this step is attached as the second picture file.

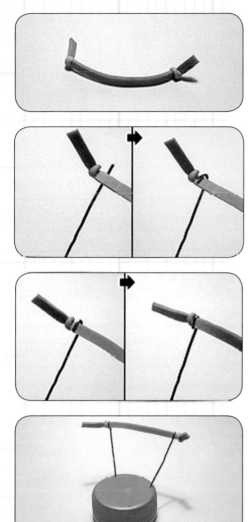

Step 7: Bend the Two New Arms

These two arms are what are going to hold the firing latch in place, so they need to be bent closer together, and then have a loop made on the top of each. You may find that before making the loops, you need to cut about ½ centimeter off the top of the arms, just to ensure that it is at half the height of the arms holding the rubber bands. Do not fully close the loops as you will need to slip the latch through them.

Step 6: Bend the Other Paperclip and Push into Bottle Cap

Exactly like Step 4, bend a paper clip, but this time leave a 1.5 cm gap in the middle. Then push it through the two remaining holes.

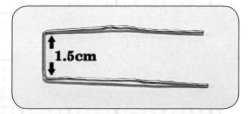

95

Step 8: Making the Firing Latch

This is the part of the booby trap that hooks onto the stretched rubber band until the trip wire is pulled. You create this by bending your last paper clip in half, bending the end so that it forms a hook, and then bending the two ends in on each other. You can then attach it to the empty arms and tighten the loops you created in the last step. View the pictures below to gain a full understanding of what you need to do with the paper clip. To adjust the sensitivity of your booby trap, you simply change the angle of the hook.

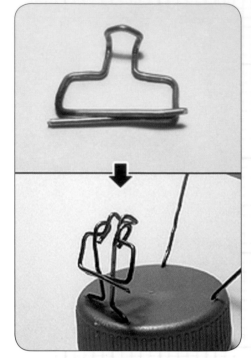

Step 9: Attaching the Trip Wire

The trip wire is used to make the latch raise, thus releasing the rubber band. The trip wire is attached by making two holes in the bottle top—one on the top underneath the latch and the other below it on the side. Then feed the wire through the string and tie it to the center of the latch.

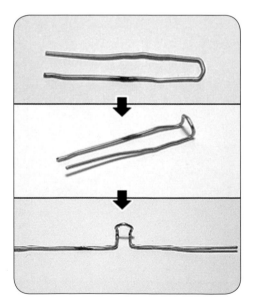

miscellaneous

Step 10: Fixing It Down

When you set your booby trap, you are going to want to stop it from moving about and remove the possibility of it being pulled over by the trip wire. To give you the ability to fix it down, make 4 holes—two on one side of the bottle top and two on the other. Then, thread some string through the holes and tie a knot. All you need do now in order to fix your booby trap in place is to either tape the string down or use the two drawing pins like in the picture below. This also gives it the ability to be fixed to a vertical surface.

Step 11: Finished! Try It Out!

It is now time to test your booby trap.

To load your booby trap, simply pull back the rubber band and hook it on the latches hook. Then put whatever projectile you wish in front of the rubber band. You'll be surprised how far it shoots the object.

miscellaneous

Desktop Skeeball

By fungus amungus
(http://www.instructables.com/
id/Desktop-Skeeball/)

I love Skeeball, but it's not often I can get my fix. So instead of trying to get out to the local bar that has a machine, I decided to just make a small one with some cardboard, coffee cups, and hot glue.

It actually works pretty well and came together in about an hour. Check it out.

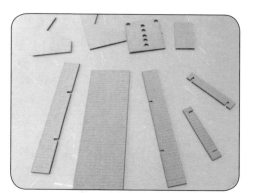

Step 1: Cutting Up the Cardboard

I'm using ⅓in ball bearings as balls, so I scaled everything around that, making this a 1:9 scale of the full size machine.

With the file handy, I cut all the pieces out on our Epilog laser cutter. I know, I know, you don't have one of your own; but with an X-acto, you can cut everything up just fine. For the holes, you can maybe use a drill.

Step 2: Assembling the Ramp

The base of the ramp is made by connecting the two cross pieces with the

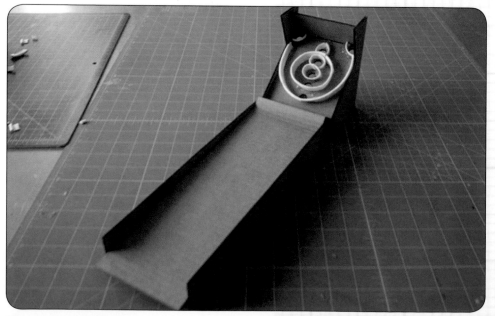

two side pieces and using some hot glue to keep it strong.

For the ramp piece itself, I used an X-acto to slice lines across the back so that the front would have a smoother curve to it. After this was done, I used the body of the X-acto as a guide for the curvature of the ramp.

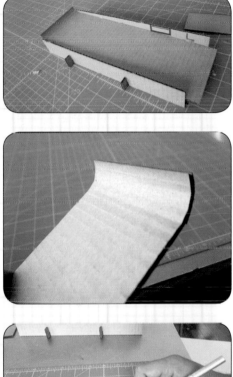

Step 3: Target

I did this a bit out of order. I should've added the rings before assembling this. Ah well, here's what I did.

I glued the two center pieces together first, keeping them at a right angle to each other. Then, I glued the side pieces on one at a time. No real advice for this, just try and keep it even and you'll be fine.

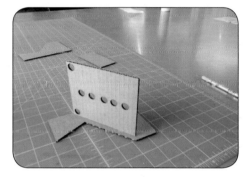

Step 4: Cutting Out Ring Material

I needed some rings to guide the balls into the drops, so I cut off the tops of a few coffee cups. To make sure they were roughly the same size, I used one cup as a guide while I cut the other one.

Step 5: Attach rings

Keep trimming off ring material until you get pieces that are the right size and glue them down. I was able to use a staple to hold the 20 point ring (the biggest circle), but for everything else it was mostly a matter of putting in a drop of hot glue, placing the ring, and holding it in place until it cooled and stuck.

And there you go! You have your own desktop skeeball set. Just place the cut off bottom of a coffee cup under the target to collect the balls and you're ready to rock.

Enjoy!

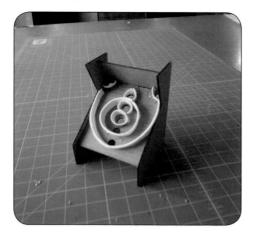

Step 6: Future Changes

My goal for this project was to see what I could make in an hour. The results are good for goofing off for a couple minutes at a time and I'm happy with it, but of course it could do with some changes. Here's a list of things that could be modified in the future.

Ball launcher: A spring-loaded plunger, like on a pinball table, would be great for shooting balls. It gives you more control of the shot. I tried a few ways to user rubber bands, but it never worked very well. It's too easy for the band to snap under the ball.

Narrower ramp: The ramp doesn't need to be as wide as the target area, and in fact this makes it easier to go off the side. Looking back at the pictures of the arcade machine, I found that the ramp is indeed narrower with one side used for the ball return.

Plastic walls: A clear acrylic side to the target area would be cool, so you can see more of what's happening from more of an angle.

Score chutes: Make chutes so that the balls fall into them after going through the holes. These can lead to a collection area that holds them in different sections and lets you see what your score is.

Ball return: An alternative to the chutes, the ball return could simply be an angled piece of cardboard underneath the target area that rolls the balls back at you.

miscellaneous

Duct Tape Boomerang

By smileys
(http://www.instructables.com/
id/Duct-Tape-Boomerang/)

I have been trying to make a really good boomerang for a while now. I have made successful wooden boomerangs, but they would always break after a few good hard hits on the pavement. So I decided that I would make a more resilient boomerang. This duct tape boomerang's strength lies in the fact that it can bend without breaking and the fact that it is waterproof. This boomerang, if given a proper throw and if made correctly, will come back to you (unless it is too windy). Keep in mind that this may take some practice.

Notes:
- This is not made out of 100 percent duct tape.
- For this instructable it really helps if you already know how to throw a working boomerang.
- It works in little to no wind only.
- In hot weather, the boomerang often becomes quite flimsy, and will most likely not work.

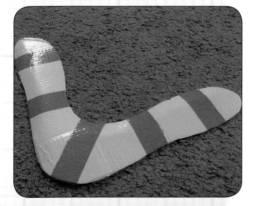

Step 1: Materials and Tools
- Duct tape (I used colored duct tape.)
- Flexible cutting boards (You can buy a pack of three at Wal-mart for $3 to $4, and each board can fit 4 to 5 boomerangs.)
- Scissors

Step 2: Make an Outline for Your Boomerang and Cut It Out

Now you need to draw the outline for your boomerang. I have found that the L-shaped boomerangs work best. I would not make a boomerang bigger than the one in the pictures below. The angle isn't too important. I would say 50–110 degrees for the angle is good. Also you don't want to make the wings to thin.

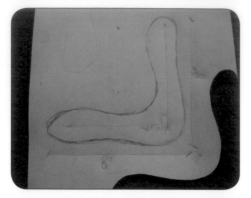

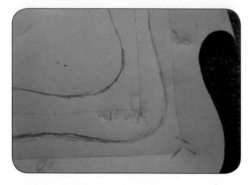

usually 2 to 3 layers of duct tape on either side, 4 to 6 layers total, will do it.) To find out how thick you need it, start by adding two layers of duct tape, and test it (see next step); if it ends up needing more, just add more until it is perfect. (Although in the pictures the duct tape overlaps in the corner of the boomerang, I have found out that having some of the layers not overlap helps to keep the boomerang lighter and better balanced, thus improving its functionality.)

Next, bend the boomerang's wings to make the airfoils. See the picture with the orange and white striped boomerang to see which way to put the airfoils. (The airfoils in the picture are for people who throw with their right hand. If you throw with your left hand, just make all the airfoils go the other way.)

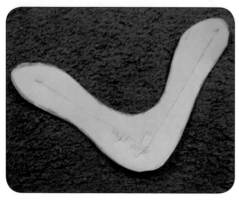

Step 3: Adding Duct Tape and Making the Airfoils

Start by adding one strip of duct tape across one of the wings, and do the same on the other wing. Now, add the duct tape in the same way but on the back of the boomerang. Go ahead and cut off the excess duct tape. Keep on adding and cutting the duct tape until it is the desired thickness. (This varies on the boomerang; however,

miscellaneous

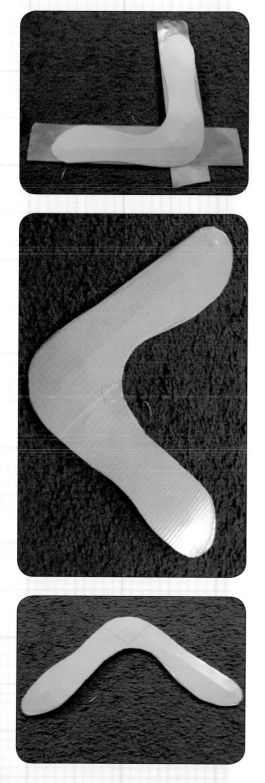

Step 4: Testing

For this step it helps to have experience throwing a working boomerang.

If your boomerang isn't working, it is probably one or a combination of these four things:

1. You aren't throwing it right (not putting the right amount of spin or/ and power, throwing it at the wrong angle, etc.)
2. Your boomerang design isn't working (wings could be too small or too big, or it could be the shape or pattern).
3. It is too heavy, in which case remove some duct tape.
4. It is too light, in which case add more duct tape

If it works however, decorate (if you want) and have fun!

Step 5: Decorate (Optional)

Use different colored duct tapes and permanent markers to decorate your boomerang (see pictures).

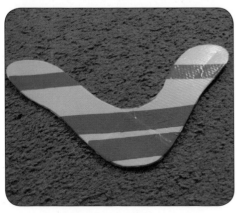

How to Make a Shuriken out of a CD

By i am cool 101
(http://www.instructables.com/
id/How-to-make-a-Shuriken-out-
of-a-CD/)

Do you ever wish that you could own a Shuriken that can fly like the one Naurto used? Well, you can own one right now for under $10! WARNING: This is a Shuriken that can still hurt people or living things (even though the edges aren't that sharp). Please don't throw it at people. It's not my fault if you want to be a fool.

Step 1: Tools and Materials

- An old CD
- A roll of scotch tape
- A knife-grinder
- A permanent marker
- A pair of scissor
- A ruler
- Some sand paper
- Silver, black, or gray paint

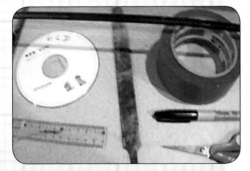

Step 2: Taping the CD

Cover the CD with Scotch tape on both sides about three times. Doing this will prevent the CD from breaking after you cut it.

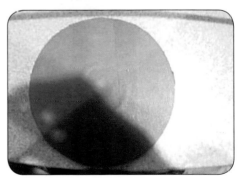

Step 3: The Shape—Part 1

Now, take your marker and ruler and you're ready for the third step. Use the ruler and draw a cross on the taped CD (as shown in the picture). Make sure the corners are 90°. Next, turn the CD so the cross looks like an X, and draw a dot

105

in the middle with a distance of 1.5 cm from the center (or in the middle of a 90° angle; look at all the pictures).

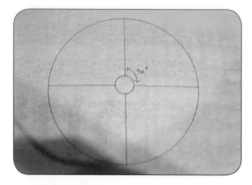

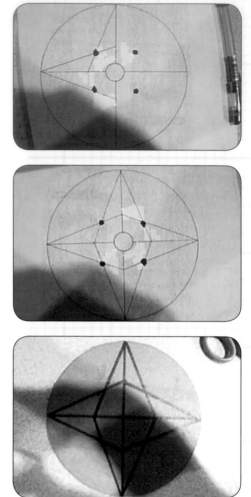

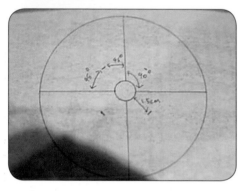

Step 4: The Shape—Part 2

Now, draw a line from the tip of a line of the cross (or X) and pass it through the dot, not passing the other line of the cross. Each dot will be passed by only two lines. Repeat for the rest and you should be finished with the shape. Look at the pictures for a better understanding.

Step 5: Cutting the CD

Follow the lines, and cut the unneeded parts out with a big scissor (like I did in the picture). Be careful, the CD might break during the cutting. If it does, just put some more tape on it.

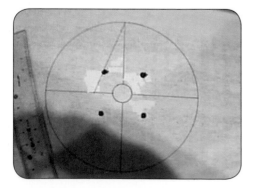

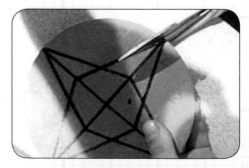

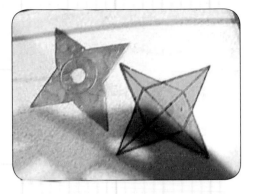

Step 6: Sharpening the Edges

Take your knife-grinder and start grinding the shuriken on the edges so it looks like it's sharp. Do it to every edge and also the back.

Step 7: The Painting

For the last step, put the shuriken on a piece of paper and paint one side at a time. After one side has dried, paint the other side. After one day, you can use it. Now, go out and use it!

Paper Nunchakus
By imthereal
(http://www.instructables.com/
id/Paper-Nunchakus/)

This Instructable will provide you with nunchakus to practice with. They still hurt but they aren't anything serious. It's not my fault if you injure or kill yourself or someone else with these. Please have common sense. They are made from:

- 2 magazines without thick spines (I used Boys Life)
- Duct tape
- 3 feet of nylon rope or twine

Step 1: Preparing the Magazines

You need two magazines, preferably both with around fifty pages. The magazines need to not have thick spines. It works best if the pages are just stapled together at the end instead of glued next to each other. Roll up a magazine as tight as you can but leave enough of a hole in the middle that you could slip a small rope into the inside. Hold it upright and make the edges even by placing the bottom on a table and pushing down on the top. Once it is even, tape the sides on the top and bottom to get it to hold its position. Repeat.

Step 2: Wrapping the Magazines

Grab a roll of duct tape and cut five or six 4" sections. Take one and wrap it straight across your magazine. Take another section of tape and do the same thing, going straight across the magazine but lower down and slightly overlapping the previous section of tape. Continue down until you get to the bottom. Do the same thing with the other magazine.

Step 3: Inserting the Rope

Collect a 3' section of nylon rope; if you don't have any, twine will work too, but it won't be as nice. Push the rope through the hole you were supposed to leave in the magazine until it comes out the other side. if your hole is too small,

then you can use all those cool Get the Rope Through Tricks you should know, like attaching a weight to the end to help pull it through, or if you can reach it, needle-nose pliers. Anyway, get the rope through to the other side, tie a double granny knot in the end of it, and pull it to the end of the magazine so it is tight. Tie just a single knot on the long side of the rope, also hugging the magazine. Tie two more single knots right next to the other, within a half inch or so. Put the other magazine on your rope and tie a double granny hugging the end of it. Cut off your extra rope and you're done. Have fun and don't die.

The Quick and Dirty Electric Tripwire

By Scissorman
(http://www.instructables.com/
id/Office-Supplies-Challenge-
The-Quick-and-Dirty-elec/)

This is like my previous tripwire Instructable but from items found around the office.

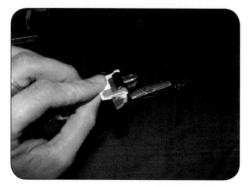

Step 1: Tools and Materials

* Bulldog clip
* String
* Foil (from your sandwich perhaps)
* Blu-tac k
* Crocodile clips
* Wire
* Device you want to turn on

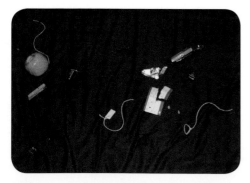

Step 2: Constructing the Switch

Cut off a bit of card big enough to fill the jaws of the clip once folded in half and then some. You don't want the crocodile clips touching the metal bulldog clip as that would be rubbish. Fold it in half. Take the foil (I folded it in half for strength but a strip of tape would work better) and attach to one half of the card with Blu-tack or double-sided tape. Try to place it so that it receives the most pressure from the bulldog clip. The metal needs to be exposed. Leave enough hanging out the side to attach the crocodile clips to. Repeat on the other side, making sure that, when folded, they touch and that the overhang is on the other side.

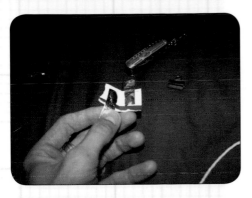

Step 3: Making the Anchor Line

You need to make an anchor line. Don't add the string to the clip. It'll probably just cause the guts to get pulled out when it gets tripped. Make a loop around your card and insert that into the clip. That should hold it all together a lot better.

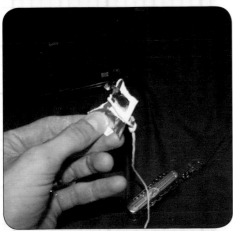

Step 4: The trip Mechanism

Add a hole to card. Tie string through the hole (the longer trip wire string). Make sure the card is wide enough to prevent any shorts within the trip switch.

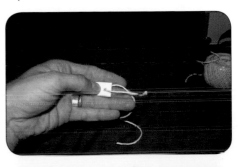

Step 5: And Finally . . .

Clamp the trip mechanism in between the foiled card with the bulldog clip. Tie off the anchor securely and the trip wire securely across the path you want to arm. Crocodile clips attach to the foil pads and, from there, to anything you want. I don't recommed the quick and dirty squib for inside use but the choice is yours.

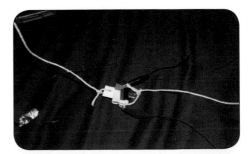

Zip Tie Ball
By alejandroerickson
(http://www.instructables.com/
id/Zip-Tie-Ball/)

This ball is made from zip ties and has a nice mathematical coloring.

You will need:
- 60 small zip ties (zap straps, plastic cable ties). Large zip ties are more difficult to hack for this project.
- A push pin
- Needle nose pliers
- Tester's model paint (optional)

If you are math inclined, we are building a dodecahedron with a five-coloring that shows its rotational symmetry group, A5. That is, all 60 even permutations of the five colors can be obtained by rotating the zip-tie ball about a pair of opposite faces (diamonds, triangles, or rounded pentagons).

Many different shapes can be built with this method.

Step 1: Make zip tie triangles
Attach three zip ties together in a loop, pulling the heads half way onto the "zippers." Now repeat that 20 times.

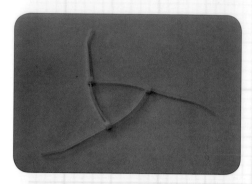

Step 2: Connect triangles
This is the secret step to connect two triangles: Stuff the thin tail from one triangle into a zip tie head on another triangle.

First, you need to decide which way your triangles go; clockwise or counterclockwise. Whichever it is, take note of which side of the triangle will be inside the Zip Tie Ball. This is important because it will give the ball a more uniform curvature.

Use a push pin to widen a head's hole, above the existing zip tie inserted through it, on the edge near the inside of the ball.

Hold the head and zip tie firmly in place while you remove the push pin.

Insert a zip tie tail of another triangle into the head, keeping the same orientation and direction as the

miscellaneous

original zip tie. Use the push pin to coax it through if you need to.

When you can get hold of it, pull it through with needle nose pliers until just before the zipper part enters the head.

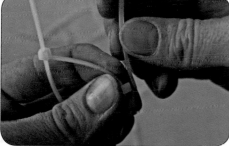

Step 3: Building patterns

Congratulations, you have learned the basic step. Now if you do that 60 times in the right places, you'll have a Zip Tie Ball!

The Zip Tie Ball has 12 circles each made of five triangles (faces of the dodecahedron). We'll start with one circle and build from there.

Notice that each pair of adjacent triangles is attached at two places, forming a little diamond between them. Be careful that all your triangles are oriented the same way you chose in Step 2!

Don't just build 12 of circles. Build onto the first one instead, and close circles when they have five triangles.

Step 4: Build onto the first circle

Your first circle has five tails, so attach a triangle to each one. The great thing about this shape is that it is mathematically impossible to mess it up (but human error will almost surely thwart your first effort). As long as you follow the instructions when attaching new triangles, and all your circles have exactly five triangles around them, you cannot end up with the wrong shape (I may regret saying this). That said, I'll give you a few more pointers:

Always connect everything that should be connected before adding a new triangle to the zip tie ball.

Be very methodical. After making the first circle, extend each tail by one triangle. Then extend one of those by one triangle, and close the new circle that has five triangles. Now do another one, etc.

Double check things often. Are your circles exactly five triangles around? Is there something else you can connect? Should you add a new triangle, or connect existing ones?

Good luck on this part!

If you want to make different shapes, make circles with different numbers of triangles around them. You will likely need a different number of zip ties if you do that.

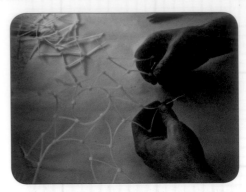

Step 5: Finish the construction

After you've closed half of the circles, most of the building is finished.

Now extend each tail by a triangle (I might have broken one of my rules here), and then attach them together to form the final circle, as well as close the five circles adjacent to it.

YOU ARE DONE WITH THE CONSTRUCTION!

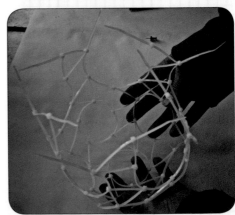

miscellaneous

Step 6: How to color the Zip Tie Ball with "A5"

You only need to know how to add one color. If you follow the same instructions for all 5, they will never interfere with each other! When I say "color a diamond," you can take that to mean, "color part of a diamond" as long as you are consistent for every diamond.

Pick a color and use the same one for all these steps.

Color an uncolored diamond.

Color the diamond opposite this diamond.

Imagine the Zip Tie Ball is the Earth, and the colored diamonds are the North and South Poles. The Equator passes through exactly four more diamonds (also opposite pairs).

Color the diamonds on the equator.

Follow these steps with each of 5 different colors. Tester's model paints worked nicely for me, but I don't know whether they will remain stretchy over time, which is desirable because the Zip Tie Ball is bouncy.

Step 7: Color in the "fill" and learn about the symmetry group

Color the remaining parts of the Zip Tie Ball with a neutral "color." Congratulations, you are finished! Now make yourself some coffee and learn about the beautiful coloring we used.

This coloring is very special because it shows off the symmetry group of the shape. A symmetry of a shape is a pair of distinct positions that look the same. You've probably heard of mirror symmetry, since your face has left-right mirror symmetry, but that's exactly the kind we won't think about here. We are talking about 3D rotational symmetry. For example a pencil has six-way cyclic rotational symmetry. There are six positions of the pencil that look the same because they are rotations of each other (assuming the pencil has no markings). Each shape has exactly one symmetry group.

The symmetry group of a shape is the set 3D rotations that take the shape from a given position, to all those that are symmetric to it. For a pencil this is a rotation around the length of the pencil through 1/6, 2/6, 3/6, 4/6, 5/6 and 6/6 of a full rotation. We call this the cyclic group on six elements.

For the Zip Tie Ball it is more complicated, so we abstract the essential information to describe the symmetry group in terms of five, colors which I call 1, 2, 3, 4, and 5. If we take the colors 12345 to be those that are clockwise around one of the circles, starting at the noon position (from wherever we are viewing the shape), we can rotate the Zip Tie Ball clockwise around that circle to make it show 51234. And then again to get 45123, and again 34512, and again 23451, and again 12345. We have already discovered a subgroup, and it is the cyclic group on six elements!

There are other symmetries which map circles to circles, and they are all a special kind of permutation of the original 12345, called an even permutation. It's nice that our colors are numbered, because an even permutation of 12345, is one that has an even number of digits that are out of order; that is, the larger one is on the left. For example 51342 has six pairs of digits out of order (51,53,54,52,32,42), so it is an even permutation. The even permutations of 12345 make up exactly half of all possible permutations, which total 120. Therefore our Zip Tie Ball has exactly 60 symmetries!

Here is a nice introduction to alternating groups for math students:

Let's go back to where we rotated around a circle. After five steps, we came back to where we started at 12345. Since these 1/5 circular rotations that we made brought us back to the start after being applied 5 times, we call this an element (3D rotation) of order 5. We can make 1/3 circular rotations around a triangle to get an element of order 3, and 1/2 circular rotations around a diamond are of order 2. These circular rotations can be combined.

So what does a 1/3 clockwise rotation do to 12345? Now we really need to use the Zip Tie Ball. First decide which colors will be 12345. I've chosen red, blue, purple, yellow, and green in the photo. If we rotate 1/3 clockwise around the triangle directly beneath it, the colors 12345 are replaced with purple, blue, yellow, red, green or 32415. The colors not touching the triangle (2 and 5) have not changed position!

Now check out the 1/2 rotations around diamonds yourself! Can you get 3D rotations of any other order by combining different cyclic (circular) rotations?

Another exercise: What happens to the colors around other circles when you rotate around a circle. For example, if I rotate around the circle 12345, through to 51234, what happened to the colors on the circle 32415?

Not satisfied? Don't forget that it bounces!

CONVERSION TABLES

One person's inch is another person's centimeter. Instructables projects come from all over the world, so here's a handy reference guide that will help keep your project on track.

Measurement									
	1 Millimeter	1 Centimeter	1 Meter	1 Inch	1 Foot	1 Yard	1 Mile	1 Kilometer
Millimeter	1	10	1,000	25.4	304.8	—	—	—
Centimeter	0.1	1	100	2.54	30.48	91.44	—	—
Meter	0.001	0.01	1	0.025	0.305	0.91	—	1,000
Inch	0.04	0.39	39.37	1	12	36	—	—
Foot	0.003	0.03	3.28	0.083	1	3	—	—
Yard	—	0.0109	1.09	0.28	033	1	—	—
Mile	—	—	—	—	—	—	1	0.62
Kilometer	—	—	1,000	—	—	—	1.609	1

Volume									
	1 Mil-liliter	1 Liter	1 Cubic Meter	1 Tea-spoon	1 Tablespoon	1 Fluid Ounce	1 Cup	1 Pint	1 Quart	1 Gallon
Milliliter	1	1,000	—	4.9	14.8	29.6	—	—	—	—
Liter	0.001	1	1,000	0.005	0.015	0.03	0.24	0.47	0.95	3.79
Cubic Meter	—	0.001	1	—	—	—	—	—	—	0.004
Teaspoon	0.2	202.9	—	1	3	6	48	—	—	—
Tablespoon	0.068	67.6	—	0.33	1	2	16	32	—	—
Fluid Ounce	0.034	33.8	—	0.167	0.5	1	8	16	32	—
Cup	0.004	4.23	—	0.02	0.0625	0.125	1	2	4	16
Pint	0.002	2.11	—	0.01	0.03	0.06	05	1	2	8
Quart	0.001	1.06	—	0.005	0.016	0.03	0.25	.05	1	4
Gallon	—	0.26	264.17	0.001	0.004	0.008	0.0625	0.125	0.25	1

conversion tables

Mass and Weight						
	1 Gram	1 Kilogram	1 Metric Ton	1 Ounce	1 Pound	1 Short Ton
Gram	1	1,000	—	28.35	—	—
Kilogram	0.001	1	1,000	0.028	0.454	—
Metric Ton	—	0.001	1	—	—	0.907
Ounce	0.035	35.27	—	1	16	—
Pound	0.002	2.2	—	0.0625	1	2,000
Short Ton	—	0.001	1.1	—	—	1

Speed		
	1 Mile per hour	1 Kilometer per hour
Miles per hour	1	0.62
Kilometers per hour	1.61	1

Temperature		
	Fahrenheit (°F)	Celsius (°C)
Fahrenheit	—	(°C x 1.8) + 32
Celsius	(°F − 32) / 1.8	—

also available

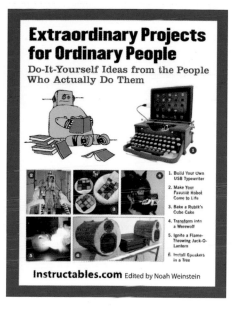

Extraordinary Projects for Ordinary People
Do-It-Yourself Ideas from the People Who Actually Do Them
by Instructables.com, edited by Noah Weinstein

Collected in this volume is a best-of selection from Instructables, reproduced for the first time outside of the web format, retaining all of the charm and ingenuity that make Instructables such a popular destination for Internet users looking for new and fun projects designed by real people in an easy-to-digest way.

Hundreds of Instructables are included, ranging from practical projects like making a butcher-block countertop or building solar panels to fun and unique ideas for realistic werewolf costumes or transportable camping hot tubs. The difficulty of the projects ranges from beginner on up, but all are guaranteed to raise a smile or a "Why didn't I think of that?"

US $16.95 paperback ISBN: 978-1-62087-057-0

How to Do Absolutely Everything
Homegrown Projects from Real Do-It-Yourself Experts
by Instructables.com, edited by Sarah James

Continuing the Instructables series with Skyhorse Publishing, a mammoth collection of projects has been selected and curated for this special best-of volume of Instructables. The guides in this book cover the entire spectrum of possibilities that the popular website has to offer, showcasing how online communities can foster and nurture creativity.

From outdoor agricultural projects to finding new uses for traditional household objects, the beauty of Instructables lies in their ingenuity and their ability to find new ways of looking at the same thing. *How to Do Absolutely Everything* has that in spades; the possibilities are limitless, thanks to not only the selection of projects available here, but also the new ideas you'll build on after reading this book. Full-color photographs illustrate each project in intricate detail, providing images of both the individual steps of the process and the end product.

US $16.95 paperback ISBN: 978-1-62087-066-2

also available

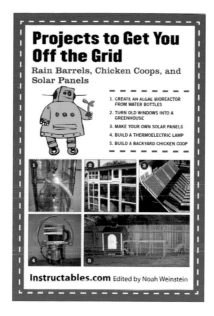

Projects to Get You Off the Grid
Rain Barrels, Chicken Coops, and Solar Panels
by Instructables.com, edited by Noah Weinstein

Instructables is back with this compact book focused on a series of projects designed to get you thinking creatively about thinking green. Twenty Instructables illustrate just how simple it can be to make your own backyard chicken coop or turn a wine barrel into a rainwater collector.

Illustrated with dozens of full-color photographs per project accompanying easy-to-follow instructions, this Instructables collection utilizes the best that the online community has to offer, turning a far-reaching group of people into a mammoth database churning out ideas to make life better, easier, and, in this case, greener, as this volume exemplifies.

US $14.95 paperback ISBN: 978-1-62087-164-5

also available

Backyard Rockets
Learn to Make and Launch Rockets, Missiles, Cannons, and Other Projectiles
by Instructables.com, edited by Mike Warren

Originating from Instructables, a popular project-based community made up of all sorts of characters with wacky hobbies and a desire to pass on their wisdom to others, *Backyard Rockets* is made up of projects from a medley of authors who have collected and shared a treasure trove of rocket-launching plans and the knowledge to make their projects soar!

Backyard Rockets gives step-by-step instructions, with pictures to guide the way, on how to launch your very own project into the sky. All of these authors have labored over their endeavors to pass their knowledge on and make it easier for others to attempt.

US $12.95 paperback ISBN: 978-1-62087-730-2

UNUSUAL USES FOR ORDINARY THINGS
250 Alternative Ways to Use Everyday Items

1. CLEAN WINDOWS WITH VODKA
2. PREVENT FIRES WITH DIAPERS
3. REMOVE RINGS WITH BUTTER
4. AVOID ODOR WITH BAKING SODA
5. SAND CURVES WITH TENNIS BALLS

instructables.com   Edited by Wade Wilgus

Unusual Uses for Ordinary Things
250 Alternative Ways to Use Everyday Items
by Instructables.com, edited by Wade Wilgus

Most people use nail polish remover to remove nail polish. They use coffee grounds to make coffee and hair dryers to dry their hair. The majority of people may also think that the use of eggs, lemons, mustard, butter, and mayonnaise should be restricted to making delicious food in the kitchen. The Instructables.com community would disagree with this logic—they have discovered hundreds of inventive and surprising ways to use these and other common household materials to improve day-to-day life.

Did you know that tennis balls can protect your floors, fluff your laundry, and keep you from backing too far into (and thus destroying) your garage? How much do you know about aspirin? Sure, it may alleviate pain, but it can also be used to remove sweat stains, treat bug bites and stings, and prolong the life of your sputtering car battery. These are just a few of the quirky ideas that appear in *Unusual Uses for Ordinary Things*.

US $12.95 paperback ISBN: 978-1-62087-725-8

also available

Practical Duct Tape Projects

by Instructables.com, edited by Noah Weinstein

Duct tape has gotten a reputation as the quick-fix tape for every situation. However, did you know that you can use duct tape to create practical items for everyday use? Did you also know that duct tape now comes in a variety of colors, so your creations can be fun and stylish? Originating from Instructables, a popular project-based community made up of all sorts of characters with wacky hobbies and a desire to pass on their wisdom to others, Practical Duct Tape Projects contains ideas from a number of authors who nurse a healthy urge to create anything possible from duct tape.

Practical Duct Tape Projects provides step-by-step instructions on a variety of useful and fun objects involving duct tape. Guided through each endeavor by detailed photographs, the reader will create articles of clothing, tools, and more.

US $12.95 paperback ISBN: 978-1-62087-709-8